CROWDSOURCE YOUR SUCCESS

How Accountability Helps You Stick to Goals

By: S.J. Scott

www.HabitBooks.com

Publishing services provided by Archangel Ink

ISBN: 1517634474
ISBN-13: 978-1517634476

Table of Contents

Disclaimer

No part of this publication may be reproduced or transmitted in any form or by any means, mechanical or electronic, including photocopying or recording, or by any information storage and retrieval system, or transmitted by email without permission in writing from the publisher.

While all attempts have been made to verify the information provided in this publication, neither the author nor the publisher assumes any responsibility for errors, omissions, or contrary interpretations of the subject matter herein.

This book is for entertainment purposes only. The views expressed are those of the author alone, and should not be taken as expert instruction or commands. The reader is responsible for his or her own actions.

Adherence to all applicable laws and regulations, including international, federal, state, and local governing professional licensing, business practices, advertising, and all other aspects of doing business in the US, Canada, or any other jurisdiction is the sole responsibility of the purchaser or reader.

Neither the author nor the publisher assumes any responsibility or liability whatsoever on the behalf of the purchaser or reader of these materials.

Any perceived slight of any individual or organization is purely unintentional.

Your Free Gift

As a way of saying *thanks* for your purchase, I'm offering a free report that's exclusive to my book and blog readers.
In *77 Good Habits to Live a Better Life*, you'll discover a variety of routines that can help you in many different areas of your life. You will learn how to make lasting changes to your work, success, learning, health and sleep habits.

Go Here to Grab 77 Good Habits to Live a Better Life:

www.developgoodhabits.com/free

PART 1

INTRODUCTION

The Importance of Accountability

"You are the sum of the five people you surround yourself with."

– Jim Rohn

Although this well-known quote has been featured in countless self-improvement books, never has there been a truer statement. The people around you often determine your level of success in life. This is true whether you want to make more money or simply lose a few pounds.

Your "inner circle" either has a positive or negative impact on what you can accomplish.

Just think of your life as it stands today. *What are your major problems? Is there anything you would like to change? Are you achieving your goals?*

Think carefully about the answers to these questions.

Odds are, your response greatly depends on the people you engage with on a regular basis. You need to take 100 percent responsibility for your life, but it's possible to predict your level of achievement by closely examining your personal network.

In the following book, **Crowdsource Your Success**, you will discover the importance of surrounding yourself with the *right* people. It doesn't matter if you'd like to improve your health, relationships *or* success in the business world. It's easier to achieve *any* goal when you add accountability to your busy schedule.

Who Am I?

My name is Steve "S.J." Scott. I run the blog Develop Good Habits, and I'm the author of a series of habit-related titles, all of which are available at HabitBooks.com.

The purpose of my content is to show how *continuous* habit development can lead to a better life. Instead of lecturing you, I provide simple strategies that are easy to use no matter how busy you get during the day.

One of the biggest lessons I've learned about habit development is that you need *accountability* to stick to a major goal. It's not enough to make a personal commitment. The big things in life require a solid action plan and a support network to tap into whenever you encounter an obstacle. This is true in the business world *and* for your personal development. When you have someone to cheer on your successes (or kick you in the butt when you're slacking), you're less likely to give up.

Without realizing it, I've had accountability in my life for over 25 years. In high school, I had a track coach and teammates who pushed me to excel at running. Later on, I participated in many informal meetups, mastermind groups and business partnerships—each focusing on a different aspect of my online business.

The past quarter-century has taught me a simple rule—the people around you *will* make or break your success.

About Crowdsource Your Success

Accountability is often perceived as a negative thing. For instance, whenever a business does something that harms the community, society looks for someone to "hold accountable." It's a term that has become synonymous with an attempt to find a scapegoat or someone to blame for a major mistake made by a company.

The truth is, accountability *can* be a positive experience. You don't have to work on your goals in isolation. Instead, you can surround yourself with people who cheer you on and coach you during those moments of doubt. To "be accountable," all you need is a clear goal and a willingness to let others help you achieve it.

There are many ways to add accountability to your life. It can be as simple as checking into a habit app on a daily basis or as challenging as being in a mastermind group that gives honest (and sometimes brutal) feedback about your goals. In *Crowdsource Your Success*, I cover all of these options and give suggestions to help you identify the strategy that works best for your personal situation.

Crowdsource Your Success is designed to integrate accountability in your everyday life without taking up a lot of your personal time.

You will learn how to:

- Identify areas of your life that would benefit from increased accountability.
- Take advantage of the different *types* of accountability, from coaches to apps to mentors.
- Form a mastermind group to receive weekly reinforcement from people who share similar goals.
- Tap into the power of networking and find the "five people" you need to have in your life.
- Track, measure and improve your progress toward major goals.
- Take consistent action—*even* if your accountability techniques are failing.
- Get continuous support for every new habit you add to your daily routine.

A goal can't be achieved in isolation, and your efforts won't always pay off in the way you expect. However, it's possible to succeed if you take the information in this book and use it to build a powerful support network of people who motivate and inspire you.

We'll cover many topics in this book, but before we dive in, I want to review what I believe to be the most important rule for maximizing your success with accountability—**Taking 100 percent responsibility for your life**. Let's get to it.

Take 100% Responsibility for Your Life

I'd like to start with a lesson I learned almost a decade ago from Jack Canfield's book, *The Success Principles: How to Get from Where You Are to Where You Want to Be.*

Although Jack covered 67 principles, he chose to start his book with this rule. When it comes to accountability, I feel it's fitting to begin the same way.

Canfield says the following:

> *"If you want to be successful, you have to take 100% responsibility for everything that you experience in your life. This includes the level of your achievements, the results you produce, the quality of your relationships, the state of your health and physical fitness, your income, your debts, your feelings—everything!"*

You might be wondering why I started this book—which is about external accountability—by talking about working on your personal issues.

Simply put, the only way you can receive the benefits of accountability is to accept the fact that everything you accomplish (or don't accomplish) in life is determined by the amount of responsibility you take.

Want to know the hard truth? In our culture (particularly in the United States), *irresponsibility* has become an epidemic. It seems like nobody is accountable for their own actions anymore.

It's always *somebody else's fault* if you're not getting the results you want.

Consider the following excuses many people use to explain their failures and mistakes:

– *"I can't find a job because of the economy."*

Perhaps the *real reason* is you never took the time to learn new skills or build a strong network in your industry.

– *"I'm always sick because food companies put salt and unhealthy sugars in their foods."*

Maybe you should take the time to educate yourself on healthy nutrition and learn how to fully understand food labels.

– *"The bank foreclosed on my house. It's their fault because they said I qualified for a loan that I couldn't afford."*

The real reason is you didn't take the time to evaluate your financial situation and figure out how much you can pay each month.

Sadly, these excuses are very common in our society. We have become a group of people who often play the "blame game" whenever something goes wrong.

Look at it this way…

I guarantee that you probably blame someone else for a major disappointment in your life. Think about something that went wrong. *Who do you blame?* Is it your:

- Parents
- Bosses
- Friends
- Co-workers
- Clients
- Spouses
- Religion
- Politicians
- Economic situation

Sure, we all have people in our lives who have caused us harm, but it's entirely up to you to decide how to react to these situations. If you allow people or circumstances to hold you back, then it will be nearly impossible to get any measurable results with your goals.

The point I'm trying to make is that it's time to stop the blame game and take 100% responsibility for <u>all</u> aspects of your life.

The past is the past. You can't change the way others have treated you, but you *can* change the way you react to such events. To do this, you have to give up your excuses and stop seeing yourself as a victim. You have to create a shift in your mind—*away* from blame and *toward* responsibility. This won't be a one-time shift. There will be times when you have to remind yourself to take 100% responsibility for any result you get in life.

To further illustrate this point, I want to share the formula Canfield shared in *The Success Principles*:

Events + Response = Outcome

His point is that we rarely have control over an event. What we can change is our *responses* to certain events. When you change the way you respond, you often get a completely different outcome.

Keep this principle in mind as you go through the book because there *will* be times when you want to blame others for a lack of results. But, if you carefully examine your *response* to an event, you'll see that making a different choice probably would have led to a better outcome.

How Responsibility Forms the Foundation for Accountability

There are two types of accountability—internal and external. The focus of this book is on *external* accountability, but before we get into that, it's important to understand that personal responsibility is the same thing as internal accountability.

You should always accept personal responsibility for every result, but it's often easier to blame other people (or events) in your life. Playing the "blame game" can derail your efforts at accountability because you'll struggle with understanding the relationship between taking massive action and getting results. Instead, you'll attribute every positive result to good luck and characterize every negative result as something that *just happened* to you.

When you make the decision to **be accountable**, it's essential that you *let go* of these negative thoughts and accept the fact that your future is in your hands.

There is no need to go through life making decisions based on negative events from the past.

When the next obstacle comes along, don't let it stop you. Instead, focus on staying positive and taking action to move forward.

Albert Einstein gave us a powerful quote to consider:

> *"Man must cease attributing his problems to his environment, and learn again to exercise his will – his personal responsibility."*

When you take full responsibility for everything in your life, an amazing thing happens. You stop worrying about every event and start consistently asking yourself a simple but important question:

"What can I do right now to make progress on this goal?"

You don't have to worry about answering this question right away. Later on, I'll show you how the different types of accountability can help you make serious progress toward any of your goals.

Before we talk about that, let's dive into the benefits of accountability and cover why this strategy should become an important part of your personal development.

PART II

THE ACCOUNTABILITY ADVANTAGE

7 Benefits of the Accountability Strategy

You might think it seems like a lot of extra work to worry about accountability and interacting with others as you work on goals. Perhaps you think it's busywork that doesn't have value in the real world. But, as Peter Drucker once said, "what gets measured, gets managed."

In other words, the primary benefit of accountability is you will achieve (or stick with) a goal when you receive constant feedback from others.

Beyond that, there are many other reasons why accountability has such a positive impact on personal development. In this section, I'll go over seven primary benefits.

Benefit #1: You perform better under observation.

People make better choices and perform at a higher level when they know they are being watched by others. The reasoning is simple—when you are held accountable for your actions, you will work harder.

Just think about your own life...

Odds are, you've probably had an exercise routine at some point. When you worked out in front of others, didn't you push just a little harder? You knew people were watching, so you tried to look your best in front of them. You might have lifted heavier weights or ran a little faster on the treadmill.

When you worked out at home, on the other hand, it was easier to take a break or not do an extra set because no one was there to push you.

This phenomenon has been proven by hundreds of psychological tests over the course of the last sixty years.

The most famous example is the Hawthorne effect, also known as the "observer effect," which states that you'll probably do a better job when someone is watching you perform a task.

The term "Hawthorne effect" was coined by Henry A. Landsberger in 1950. Landsberger was analyzing experiments conducted between 1924 and 1932 at the Hawthorne Works, a Western Electric factory near Chicago. The factory had commissioned the study to see if workers would be more productive in higher or lower levels of light.

The researchers noticed that the workers' productivity *improved* when the study began and *slumped* when it ended.

In the end, the researchers suggested that the workers' increase in productivity was the direct result of being under the watchful eyes of outside observers.

In the sixty years since this experiment, the same idea has been tested again and again, always yielding the same results—being observed while you perform an activity <u>will</u> help you perform better.

Remember, accountability requires two parts: internal control *and* external support.

Being personally responsible for your results is important, but it's not enough to achieve peak performance. You need that external accountability to keep you on track.

Benefit #2: You get honest feedback from others.

Asking questions is one of the best ways to get feedback on a specific goal. Everyone views the world differently because our "lens" is tinted by our own experiences, knowledge and education.

The things we believe are common sense are often not fully understood by others. With external accountability, you consistently have people in your life who ask: *"Why is this important?"* or *"How does this action relate to your goal?"* Being challenged like this is a good thing because it forces you to closely examine each goal and make sure it's your best course of action.

To illustrate this point, let's look at two examples of how the right questions can help you achieve breakthrough success:

Online Business (Example 1)

You are determined to start an online business. You've watched a friend achieve massive success, so you set a goal to follow the same path.

Right now, you might be considering a new, but expensive, course that's supposed to teach you the fundamentals of a particular business.

With accountability, you will have people who can ask important questions like these:

- How do you know this program is the right program? Do you know someone who has taken the course?
- Have you read reviews? Are they positive or negative?
- Do you have the necessary skills and budget to help you realistically accomplish goals related to your new business?
- What do you like about the idea of owning your own online business? Besides the story of your successful friend, what makes you believe this business is right for you?

There are many pitfalls when it comes to running an online business, plus there are numerous scam artists who are more than happy to sell you bogus products that rarely work. The benefit of accountability is you'll have someone there to provide a reality check whenever you're about to make a major purchase.

Fitness (Example 2)

Let's say you are tired of being out of shape (or overweight) and you are ready to make an immediate change. You found a new video series that promises to get you in amazing shape in 90 days. It requires you to purchase new equipment plus a series of videos. You are willing to do whatever it takes to meet your fitness goals, but you're not sure if you should invest in these items.

With accountability, you can get valuable feedback from others. People in your support network might ask challenging questions like these:

- Have you checked with your doctor to make sure you're healthy enough to begin such an intense workout?
- Do you have the money set aside to make this purchase?
- Do you have space in your home for the new equipment?
- Are you worried you might get burned out with such an intense workout right as you begin your fitness journey?

It's easy to get overwhelmed by all of the steps required to achieve a new goal. Fortunately, you can get answers to many of your questions by surrounding yourself with people who are knowledgeable enough to provide honest advice about what you need to do.

Benefit #3: Accountability forces you follow through on commitments.

We are all human, and, as such, it's easy to make mistakes. You might start working toward a new goal and have every intention of following through with it, but rarely does that good feeling last more than a few days. You usually get sidetracked by "life" and quickly forget about continuing with your goal.

Stop to consider your own life for a moment. How many times have you set a goal, started to work on it and then quit a few days later? From half-completed housing projects to that "extreme" exercise program advertised on television, we've all experienced high levels of motivation that are quickly followed by a change in attitude.

There are many reasons it's hard to stick to a new routine; however, one of the main reasons you don't follow through is because you lack of accountability.

To illustrate this point, let's talk about a principle called "implementation intention," a concept psychologist Peter Gollwitzer came up with in the mid-'90s.

In one experiment, Gollwitzer asked his students to mail in an assignment two days before Christmas. One group was given the assignment with no additional instructions, while the other was asked to form specific if-then statements: *When* they would mail it, *where* they would mail it and *how* they would mail it.

The results were as follows:

- The first group (who had no specific instructions) had a 32 percent success rate.
- The second group (who had if-then instructions) had a 72 percent success rate.

By taking the time to create a plan, the people in the second group more than doubled their success rate.

All Gollwitzer really did was provide the "if-then group" with a bit of accountability to follow through with their goals. The lesson here is that you are more likely to achieve your goals when you make other people aware of them.

Accountability also provides an opportunity to identify potential obstacles and create a plan for avoiding them.

The students involved in Gollwitzer's experiment recognized the potential pitfalls associated with the project: being too busy with other assignments, getting sidetracked by outside distractions, or even pure laziness. By forming if-then statements, the students were able to clearly identify what *might* prevent them from completing the assignment and then adjust accordingly.

Consider another example of using if-then statements to meet your goals.

Let's assume your goal is to stop wasting money. It's difficult to turn this goal into a daily habit, so it's a real challenge for most people. In fact, focusing on *not* spending money is often counterproductive. That's because the act of trying to not do something often makes you want to engage in the activity even more than usual.

When it comes to a nebulous goal like "stop wasting money," you'd be better off identifying the triggers that cause you to overspend and creating a series of if-then plans to overcome them.

You could do this in a few ways:

- If I go to the mall, then I will avoid the shoe store.
- If I end up in the shoe store, then I will not buy anything.
- If I go to Amazon, then I will only buy things I need.
- If I go out dancing, then I will avoid buying expensive drinks.
- If I go shopping for Christmas presents, then I will stick to a budget.

If-then planning can be a part of your internal accountability, but it's *more* effective as a part of your external accountability.

A study from the Dominican University of California showed that goal achievement is influenced by writing goals, committing to specific actions, and being accountable for those actions through giving formal updates to others.

The study involved 267 participants recruited from businesses, organizations and networking groups.

The participants were randomly assigned to one of five groups:

- **Group 1:** Unwritten Goals
- **Group 2:** Written Goals
- **Group 3:** Written Goals and Action Commitments
- **Group 4:** Written Goals and Action Commitments to a Friend
- **Group 5:** Written Goals, Action Commitments, and Progress Reports to a Friend

Participants set personal or professional goals, then proceeded to follow the instructions for their specific group.

The researchers found that members of Group 5—the participants who wrote down their goals, committed to an action, and sent progress reports to their friends—achieved significantly more than the other groups. Group 4, with just written goals and action commitments to friends, also achieved more than Groups 1, 2, and 3.

The study provides evidence that accountability—both internal and external—is an important aspect of achieving goals.

Benefit #4: Accountability creates firm deadlines for important tasks.

Planning is an essential part of the goal-setting process, whether you're talking about a new project at work, losing 10 pounds, or building an addition to your home. Without prior planning, any task is significantly more difficult to achieve.

One essential component of planning is setting firm (and public) deadlines. Sure, keeping a private timeline in your head can work, but there is a better chance you'll follow through if you tell others about your timeline. Not only does sharing your goals keep your feet to the fire, it also forces you to finish projects by specific deadlines.

Making commitments with a public completion date has been shown to have significant advantages. Take this research article from *Psychological Science*, entitled "Procrastination, Deadlines and Performance: Self-Control by Precommitment." In the article, the authors discuss how setting deadlines and creating accountability for those deadlines are the keys to overcoming a lack of self-control and reaching your goals.

According to the authors, self-control problems arise when preferences are inconsistent across time or context.

As an example, the researchers conducted a study involving university students to test the performance of self-imposed deadlines when compared to external deadlines as precommitment mechanisms.

Students in the experimental group were given assignments with self-imposed deadlines and external deadlines. Students in the control group had no self-imposed or external deadlines. After comparing the two groups, the researchers concluded the students were better able to meet their goals when they imposed deadlines on themselves. The study also showed that results improved when there were penalties for not meeting the deadline. The authors concluded that people understand the value of binding themselves to deadlines to overcome procrastination, but the people who have external deadlines have the best chance of achieving a goal.

According to this study, your self-imposed deadlines *do* help, but it is the external deadlines—the public ones—that provide the biggest boost to your level of commitment to a goal.

Benefit #5: Accountability keeps you grounded in reality.

Being optimistic can have a positive impact on your goals. It's important to believe in yourself—even when nobody else does. However, there is a danger to having *too much* optimism. If all you do is focus on your dream, then it's easy to forget about *taking action*.

Your goals are constantly reinforced with accountability. A good network of people will keep you focused on what's important—the day-to-day tasks that often don't seem as sexy as the end goal. Sure, you might dream about what life will be like five years from now, but it's far better to get feedback like this: "Stop thinking about your five year plan. What are doing tomorrow to work on your goal?"

When looking for accountability partners, choose people who not only are encouraging, but also challenging. This will keep you grounded. Their job is to help you achieve short-term goals and big goals you won't be able to reach for several months or years.

Benefit #6: Learn from the successes and failures of others.

It's been said that failure is often our best teacher. It's not fun to make mistakes, but when you learn hard lessons, these experiences help you make better decisions down the road. That said, a major benefit of accountability is the opportunity to learn important lessons without going through the painful process of making your own mistakes.

Just talking to someone, whether it be a mentor, coach, peer, or member of a mastermind group, gives you opinions and real-life experiences to help you avoid pitfalls that would cost you time, money or a combination of both.

Accountability also makes it easier to identify challenges that you might not have initially considered. Perhaps you're too emotionally involved to predict a potential setback. It doesn't matter what your goal is; there will *always* be challenges that seem to come from nowhere.

Whether it's a snacking habit that wrecks a diet or wasting too much time on low-value business tasks, an accountability partner will often talk about what they've done wrong in the past and prevent you from making the same mistakes.

Benefit #7: Accountability prevents little problems from turning into big ones.

Little problems almost always grow into big ones unless they're immediately addressed. Sometimes you're blind to these little issues, and other times you might be willfully ignoring them.

Accountability partners often act as a second (even third or fourth) pair of eyes on your challenges. They are there to give you a kick in the butt to take care of any problem before it completely derails your progress toward a goal.

Conversely, an accountability group can encourage you to not "sweat the small stuff." It's easy to get anxious whenever you encounter an obstacle, but when you talk about an issue, a good group can help you figure out what's important to address and what can be ignored.

For instance, let's say you run an ecommerce business. During the week, there were two major issues that weighed heavily on your mind:

1) You lost a major supplier of your core product
2) You received *one* angry, ranting email from a customer (out of the thousand you get every week)

The supplier issue might seem less important because the negative consequences won't occur right away. On the other hand, the angry email seems more urgent because it feels like an emotional attack. When you talk about both issues with your mastermind group, they remind you that the email is one person's opinion and what is more important is to find another quality supplier. If you don't find a new supplier quickly, there's a chance you'll experience a serious loss in long-term revenue.

We all experience challenges, but participating in an accountability group gives you a chance to review your challenges and use member feedback to figure out where to focus your efforts.

As you can see, there are many benefits to accountability. If some of the advantages seem interesting, but you're not sure how to apply this information to real-world situations, keep reading. The next section covers a few examples of accountability and explains how people across the world use it to achieve their goals or get help with important personal issues.

Writing Groups: Most writing groups are locally based (just look in your local newspaper or on Meetup.com), but there are also forums such as <u>Writers Helping Writers</u>, <u>Writertopia</u> and <u>Writers Network</u>. By joining these sites, you can find ideas, get support and even request feedback on your writing. Connecting with other writers in this way is a great way to stay accountable for completing your writing projects.

Genealogy: Most people don't realize that accountability is an important part of genealogy. Before my aunt passed away, she and my mom used to meet and discuss their current genealogy research. Not only did this activity give the sisters a solid reason to stay connected with each other, it also gave them an opportunity to get feedback on their most recent discoveries.

There are genealogy clubs throughout the world, so the best place to look is in your own backyard. However, a great place to start is the <u>wiki page provided by Ancestry.com</u>, which has a database of national genealogy societies and the individual clubs in each U.S. state.

These are just a few examples of the skills you can improve by connecting with others who share a similar passion. Just think of any one of your goals, and you'll probably find a group that regularly meets near your home. Whether you like to sail, learn new languages or play video games, there *are* people around the world who can help you improve your skills.

Area #2: Addiction, Mental Health and Support Groups

One of the more powerful aspects of accountability is meeting with others who share the same challenges you currently face. The members of a support group can help you through rough patches and provide inspiration for the times when you feel lost.

There are addiction groups such as Alcoholics Anonymous (AA), Narcotics Anonymous, Gamblers Anonymous, Hoarders Anonymous and Sexaholics Anonymous. If you suffer from any of these issues, then you can attend a local meeting to get support from others.

If you are battling a specific disease, join a support group to connect with others going through the same thing. There are groups for people with AIDS, cancer and Alzheimer's disease, just to name a few. To find the right group, just go to Google.com and do a search in your state (or country).

Finally, there are support groups for people who want to improve their mental health. Groups are available for people with PTSD (post-traumatic stress disorder), eating disorders and different types of anxiety, among other disorders. As with the previous example, you can easily find any group by searching on Google.

You don't have to be alone with your pain. Right now, there are people who have walked the same road as you. All you have to do is take that first step forward and connect with a support group in your area.

Area #3: Diet and Weight Loss

Losing weight (and keeping it off) is a challenge for many people. Those who are successful are usually part of a support network that provides consistent, positive feedback. For instance, the following three organizations provide lots of accountability for their members:

Weight Watchers: This international company offers meetings in most cities and towns in the United States. Each local group helps you meet other people who are trying to lose weight, get a weekly weigh-in and hear from special speakers on topics related to nutrition, fitness and weight loss.

Weight Watchers also maintains an online forum for people looking to share both their successes and challenges. If you're not interested in meeting people in your area, the online forums provide resources and support similar to what you would find at a local meeting.

Jenny Craig: This is another weight-loss-management company that offers meetings in most cities and some towns in the U.S., as well as in other countries. In addition to online forums and resources, Jenny Craig offers individualized counseling both online and in person for people seeking one-on-one assistance with their efforts.

Nutrisystem: As a commercial provider of weight-loss products and services, Nutrisystem offers accountability in the form of counseling to help you reach your weight-loss goals. The program focuses on portion control, balanced nutrition and support from weight-loss counselors and dieticians to help you stay on track.

I listed these three companies *only* to give you examples of the support networks available to anyone interested in losing weight. That said, weight loss is a billion-dollar industry, which means there is a strong financial incentive to recruit members. Be sure to do your research before you sign up for any product or service.

Area #4: Fitness and Physical Improvement

Meeting with an "exercise buddy" is a classic example of accountability. We all know it's easy to blow off a solo workout, but you probably won't blow off a scheduled workout if you know someone is expecting you to show up.

Many exercise groups use this rule to their advantage, but let's focus on two:

CrossFit, a fitness company started in 2000, has taken off like wildfire. It incorporates elements of high-intensity interval training, Olympic weightlifting, plyometrics, powerlifting, gymnastics, calisthenics and strongman exercises.

The biggest selling point is CrossFit provides an *extremely* challenging workout. It's tough, but it also delivers results. Participants love the fact that it's not an activity everyone can do, so the bonds they form with other members are stronger than you see at other types of gyms.

CrossFit is a great example of accountability because participants are put into an environment where they support one another. In the 10,000 CrossFit-affiliated gyms around the world, you get coaching and accountability from staff members as well as from other CrossFit members. If anyone feels you're not working hard enough, they'll immediately let you know.

Running Clubs: Running is often perceived as a solitary activity, but in reality, many folks love the camaraderie and, of course, the accountability found in local running clubs.

The easiest way to find a local group is through the Road Runners Club of America (RRCA). If you live outside the United States, do a Google search for your country + "running club."

Running clubs offer many accountability benefits such as group runs, regular meetings, coaching sessions and meetups at local races. All of these activities create an environment that encourages you to stick with an activity that is often portrayed as boring or even grueling.

Area #5: Public Service and Volunteering

Many people may not think of volunteering as a form of accountability, but members of volunteer groups have discovered that the best way to stay committed to helping others is to join groups and meet people who share a similar passion. Here are a few examples:

Community Outreach: VolunteerMatch.org is an excellent place to start your community outreach journey. You can find volunteer opportunities related to advocacy and human rights, arts and culture, animals and much more. The VolunteerMatch website makes it easy to find local organizations in need of assistance, but there are also virtual opportunities available. Serving as a volunteer for a nonprofit gives you the chance to be part of a team and get support and accountability to help you meet your volunteering goals.

Habitat for Humanity: This well-known international nonprofit is always in need of volunteers to help build homes for people in need or for those who have gone through a natural disaster. Most major cities have a local chapter of Habitat for Humanity, making it easy to find the camaraderie and support you need. You will also have opportunities to improve your skills in areas such as organization, house building and service to others.

Hospital Volunteering: Your local hospital always needs volunteers. From checking in on patients who seem to be low in spirits to helping nurses restock supplies, you can play a vital role in providing excellent care to the hospital's patients and families. As part of a hospital volunteering group, you will get support from other volunteers and hospital staff and will likely be recognized as a cherished member of the team.

As you can see, there are opportunities all over the world for implementing accountability. Not only external accountability useful in the business world, it also helps you deal with major personal issues, tackle your next big goal and, finally, connect with people who share similar passions.

Now that you understand the *why* behind accountability, let's focus on the *how*. In the next section, we'll go over the **seven types of accountability**.

We'll cover them in the following order:

1) Mobile Apps
2) Virtual Communities
3) Accountabuddies
4) Mastermind Groups
5) Coaching
6) Mentorship
7) Conferences

I will also tell you the differences between each type of accountability, outline their advantages and disadvantages, and explain how to identify the strategy that works best for you. We'll get started with the type of accountability that is the *easiest* to implement.

Part III

7 Types Of Accountability (And How They Help With Goals)

Accountability Strategy #1

Using a Mobile App

Mobile apps provide the easiest way to get instant accountability. You won't meet with a coach face to face or keep scheduled appointments with a group. Everything is done from the comfort of your smartphone, where you track goals whenever it's convenient. This type of accountability is ideal for people who are always on the go or don't enjoy keeping a consistent schedule.

The reason we're starting with mobile apps is because this strategy will help you overcome the excuse that many people have for not being accountable. You can no longer say, *"I don't have time to track my goals," "I can't find an accountability partner"* or *"I can't afford a coach"* because this technology is easy to use and only requires five minutes of your time every day.

Whether you need help with fitness, nutrition, writing, business or life purpose, there is an accountability app that can help.

That said, it's important to remember what I said before—you should *take 100 percent responsibility* when using any app. If you don't use it every day, it's not the app's fault; it's yours! So you need to commit to the daily habit of "checking in" if you want the full benefit of this form of accountability.

The question is—Are mobile apps right for *you?*

To answer that question, here are the advantages and disadvantages of using this type of technology:

Advantages:

- The cost is minimal—sometimes even free.
- The apps are easy to find.
- You can read reviews from other users to help you make an informed decision.
- Apps are easy to download and add to your busy schedule.
- You don't have to deal with scheduling appointments or calls.
- You have the opportunity to turn accountability into a habit.
- You can use the apps everywhere you go.

Disadvantages:

- There is a low level of commitment, so if you often struggle with following through on goals, then this might not be a good option for you.
- Most apps provide very little, if any, negative or positive social approval or consequences for failing to follow through.
- For non-tech-savvy users, it can be challenging to use apps.

You will not experience the personal touch of face-to-face coaching.

While you won't get direct accountability like you do when meeting with others, mobile apps are a good place to get started. So, if you're not sure about putting yourself out there, then I recommend you check out at least one of the apps covered in the next section.

How to Pick the Right Accountability App

In one of my books, I reviewed a total of 115 apps, but I do have a few personal favorites. The following apps are specifically designed to help users identify good habits and stick with them on a daily basis.

- Coach.me: Later on, we'll talk about how this app can connect you with a coach, but its main benefit is it provides a great interface for creating habits and sticking to them. When you sign in, you'll see a list of habits with the number of participants currently committed to each one. One of the biggest benefits of using Coach.me is the support and encouragement you get from other users working toward the same goal.

- Another advantage of Coach.me is it's similar to your favorite social media sites. You can add friends, send messages, ask questions and generally support one another. This is a great example of the Hawthorne effect—users are more likely to follow through on goals when they know others are observing their behavior.

- MyFitnessPal: This popular app is designed to help users lose weight and reach their fitness goals. It features calorie counters, collects data for tracking purposes and has an active online community where you can create public accountability for your goals. In the online forum, you'll find groups categorized by topic, so it's easy to join groups based on your specific accountability needs.

- For example, there are groups for moms trying to lose baby weight and men who lift weights. There are also groups classified according to age, interests and types of workouts. There truly is a group for any interest or goal you might have.

- 21habit: *"Invest in Yourself"* is the mantra of this app, which is based on the idea that it takes 21 days to create a new habit. I tend to disagree with this assumption, because it often takes up to 66 days for a habit to stick, but I like the simple design and easy-to-use interface.

- Get started by choosing a challenge and using the app to create a new habit. Then pay $21 and check in each day for 21 days to track your progress. Each day you succeed, you get $1 back. Each day you fail, or if you don't check in for three days, you forfeit $1, which 21habit then donates to one of several charities.

- You can stop your habit or start a new habit at any time. You are also free to withdraw your remaining funds at any time. It's a fun way to stay on track and hold yourself accountable.

- Rise: The Rise nutrition app is unique because it brings personalized nutritional coaching right to your mobile device. While it's pricier than most apps, it does provide one-on-one guidance from a licensed nutrition professional. You simply fill out your personal profile, outline your goals and select a coach from the list generated by the app. You will immediately be connected with a nutritional coach via the app's messaging function.

- The app also offers a food journal and a page to view your own profile and your coach's profile. In the journal section, you log your food consumption and receive suggestions for recipes and eating times. You can also snap a photo for quick meal logging. Your coach can comment on the meal or offer modifications. This is a great tool if you are someone who really needs that external accountability to stay on track.

- Strides: This app is designed to help you maintain streaks with important habits. It's been my experience that great results often come from creating streaks with a habit. (For more on this, read this article to learn about Jerry Seinfeld's practice of writing a new joke every single day: lifehacker.com/281626/jerry-seinfelds-productivity-secret).

- Strides tracks all of your results with a simple interface that includes your target goals, milestone achievements and averages per day, week and month. You won't have to use multiple apps because all your metrics are in one central location.

- There is a monthly subscription fee for the Strides app, but it's worth the price if you're interested in tracking every aspect of your life.

Mobile apps can be an important part of your daily routine. In fact, I recommend you use them to track goals and habits—even if you choose another form of accountability covered in this section. You'll find that, once you use these apps on a regular basis, measuring every aspect of your life is rather addictive.

Now, apps are only one piece of the puzzle. The major downside of using them is it's easy to get sidetracked or bored. It's also easy to lose interest. If you want more accountability for your goals, then you'll benefit from regularly meeting and talking to people in a virtual community.

Accountability Strategy #2

Joining a Virtual Community

The benefits of mobile apps are rather limited because it's easy to ignore your device. The other strategies in this section (such as accountabuddies, coaching and mastermind groups) are limited because they require a continuous time commitment. If you're strapped for cash (or have a limited amount of time), then you might enjoy being part of a virtual community.

With a virtual community, all you need to do is log in from the comfort of your home and interact whenever you have free time. It's ideal if you want to interact with people who share a goal without being forced into a weekly commitment with strangers. It could be a great strategy for you, but it could also be a waste of time, so let's go over the advantages and disadvantages of using virtual communities for accountability.

Advantages:

- You can easily find groups based on a specific interest or goal.
- You receive decent accountability without leaving your house.
- You can check in anytime, from anywhere, to stay connected to the group.
- You meet contacts who might become lifetime friends, mentors, accountabuddies or coaches.

- You get involved in challenges and contests to hold you accountable and push you in certain areas of your life.
- You avoid spending too much of your money.

Disadvantages:

- You might not take it seriously, since you don't have any time or money invested, which often derails your ability to get accountability.
- You won't have face-to-face *live* interaction.
- You might end up in a group filled with drama or people who like to complain—even people who might steal your ideas.
- You could fall off the wagon (and forget about the group) if you hit a slump. Since there's no commitment on your part, there won't be a partner who checks in and makes sure you're staying focused.

Participating in a virtual community is a great way to get started on the path to success. Virtual communities have many resources to help you learn more about specific goals, giving you an opportunity to decide if you really want to commit to a particular course of action. Once you make the decision to commit, you can also ask community members to help you find a mastermind group.

How do you get started with virtual communities?

In the next section, I list the best websites for finding virtual communities related to a particular goal.

How to Find the Best Virtual Community

If you're not sure what I mean by a virtual community, here are a few examples. I've also given you some of the best resources for finding a group that matches your interests.

- **Forums**: You can search for online forums by topic and find vibrant groups that have a high level of interaction. Most of these groups are formed around a specific niche, so it's not too hard to find a tight-knit community of people who share a goal similar to yours.

- For example, if you are a writer, you can find plenty of writer forums, but you can also find forums for your specific writing genre. The Writer's Café section on KBoards.com, which focuses on self-publishing, is a good example.

- Google is the best way to find these groups. Simply, type forum + the goal you're trying to achieve. For instance, you could enter phrases like these: *build muscle forum, CrossFit forum* or *real estate investing forum*. Not every search result will be the right one for you, so take time to "lurk" around each forum before focusing on one (we'll talk more about this in the next section).

- **Facebook Groups**: As with forums, you can go as general or as specific as you want. Facebook features an on-site search engine to help you locate groups based on a specific topic. Some are public and some are private, but the private groups tend to be the ones where the community building happens. In many cases, all you have to do is send a brief message to the moderator explaining your interest in the topic, and they'll let you in.

- Many Facebook groups offer challenges and contests to help you work toward personal or business goals. Because Facebook is such a regular part of most people's lives, it's easy to build the habit of checking in with your groups. Not only will this help you build relationships, it will keep you accountable for working toward your goals.

- Finding a Facebook group is similar to running a search on Google. Just go to the "search Facebook" tool at the top of the page, enter a phrase related to your goal, go to the "More" option in the results and sort by Groups. The results are sorted by the number of members, so start with the first few groups to see if they're a good fit.

- **LinkedIn Groups**: Joining LinkedIn groups can fast-track your reputation as an industry expert and put you on the road to becoming an influencer in your field. LinkedIn is especially designed for building professional relationships, so it is the perfect place for developing business skills and connecting with people in your field who have goals similar to yours.

- It's easy to find groups by searching the Groups page, but you can also start your own group and invite other LinkedIn members to join.

- **Google + Communities**: All you need to search for a Google Communities group is a Google account. You can create online and email-based groups or join existing groups.

- Google Groups are similar to the groups found on Facebook and LinkedIn—you can engage in conversations, organize Hangouts, create a live event or network with members in the hopes of forming a mastermind group.

- **Brand-Specific Forums:** There are many forums built by popular bloggers, podcasters and celebrities who offer to help with specific goals. Research the top people in a specific niche, and you'll usually find they offer some type of forum or masterminding opportunity.

Membership fees vary widely from one group to another. I've seen forums cost anywhere from $5 all the way up to $197 per *month*. Obviously, you want to make sure the pricier groups will be worth the investment. The price might be worth it if you get a chance to surround yourself with action takers who consistently help one another succeed.

If you find that you're a little hesitant about jumping into a regular meeting with a mastermind group or accountabuddy, then a virtual community might be a great.

How to Get Started with Virtual Communities

Finding the *right* virtual community is as easy as scanning through a list of groups and joining the ones that seem the most interesting. My advice is to start with the social media platform you *already* use on a regular basis—like Facebook, Google+ or LinkedIn.

Here's the benefit: You've *already* created a habit of checking the site, so it won't be hard to add an extra five to 10 minutes every day to interact with members of your favorite virtual community.

I recommend you shop around before selecting a group. Look for communities with a high number of active members, many comment threads and a lot of interaction on each post. Take time to scroll through several threads to see how people treat one another. Are they providing helpful comments or leaving snide, antagonistic remarks?

Remember: The purpose of a virtual community is to be part of a positive environment, not surround yourself with negative people.

Next, you'll join a few virtual communities. Sometimes the only thing you need to do is submit an invite request; other times you have to fill out a short application. Here is where it's best to focus on quality over quantity. It's impossible to keep up with dozens of groups, so it's better to spend time building quality relationships within a handful of communities.

Once you're a member, introduce yourself, provide feedback and become an encouraging influence to others. This is quickest way to build a reputation as a valuable member of a virtual community.

Also, there's one thing to keep in mind…

Members of online groups aren't impressed when someone new joins and then immediately asks a series of repetitive questions or begs for help. It's okay to ask an occasional question, but don't be that needy person who never offers value in exchange for assistance from other members.

Finally, for best results, check in on a daily basis and respond to threads and leave comments. *When possible*, create new threads where you share an insight, link to a valuable resource or ask an open-ended question to spark conversation.

The easiest way to get used to the daily habit of interacting with a virtual community is to schedule a specific time to do so, such as in the morning before work, on your lunch break or for an hour each night before bed. Whatever time you choose, stick with it just like you would stick with a regular meeting time. When you consider this time a valuable part of your journey to accountability, you will get the most out of it.

Joining virtual communities is a great way to become comfortable with accountability. You can check in whenever you like, talk to people who share similar goals and get excellent feedback on the challenges you're currently facing. It's great to know that, whenever you need help, there is a group of people who can provide assistance.

That said, you might need a more formal arrangement involving regular meetings with another person. That's when it's time to connect with an accountabuddy.

Accountability Strategy #3

Working with an Accountabuddy

I'll admit it... *accountabuddy* sounds like an overly cute word. However, you'll find that forming this type of partnership can be one of the smartest moves you make for your personal development.

So what *is* an accountabuddy?

Simply put, it's like a partnership where you mutually agree to coach each other and provide feedback on a regular basis. You and your accountabuddy should have daily or weekly feedback sessions to share wins and talk about your current challenges.

Accountabuddy conversations have some similarity to mastermind meetings (which we'll cover next), but the biggest difference is that the flow of conversation focuses solely on the two accountabuddies instead of a group of several people. If you have an accountabuddy, you usually get more personalized help with your goals because the other person is focused on your success.

As an example, *my* accountabuddy is Tom Ewer from Leaving Work Behind. We meet on a weekly basis (except when one of us is traveling) for about 30 minutes to go over our online businesses.

This is an informal meeting where discuss our "wins" from the previous week, talk about current challenges we're facing and provide "accountability statements" (i.e. specific goals) for what we'll accomplish in the upcoming week.

The main benefit of having an accountabuddy is having ample time to talk about your specific issues. Mastermind groups are helpful, but each member has a limited amount of time to discuss challenges or share insights.

An accountabuddy isn't just useful for business owners. You can work with an accountabuddy in a variety of areas.

- Fitness training
- Diet or nutrition
- Positive self-talk or emotional growth
- Effective communication
- Relationships
- Parenting
- Smoking cessation
- Budgeting (stop wasting money or start saving)
- Home organization or cleaning
- Writing

Think of it this way—if you meet someone for a workout every single week, then you already have the foundation of a great accountabuddy partnership.

Still not sold on the concept?

Check out the advantages and disadvantages of this relationship; then decide if it sounds like something you want to try.

Advantages:

- You have an opportunity to coach someone while also receiving value in return.
- You get a very direct form of accountability. Apps are impersonal, but accountabuddies often form strong friendships as they share their hopes, struggles, dreams and goals with each other.
- You connect at a mutually convenient time. There are no appointments like you would have with a professional coach.

- Accountabuddy partnerships are usually free.

Disadvantages:

- You won't always be compatible with the person you pick. If you clash with your accountabuddy, you are likely to have arguments or major disagreements. This can be a discouraging experience or even become a major obstacle that gets in the way of your goals.
- This type of relationship is difficult to maintain if you are both busy and don't have similar schedules.
- If one accountabuddy is at a higher level than the other, the coaching can be very one-sided.
- It's not as formal as other types of accountability, which can be a distraction if you have a results-driven personality.

Working with an accountabuddy is a great option if you need constant feedback on your goals. If you're interested in finding someone to partner with, I'll show you how to get started in the next section.

How to Get Started with an Accountabuddy

The best accountabuddy arrangement is one where you meet on a regular basis (either every day or every week) and talk about your progress toward a major life goal. It doesn't have to be a long conversation—I recommend five minutes daily or 30 minutes weekly. It doesn't even have to be someone you're already friends with. In fact, it could be someone you've just met online.

During a session, you help each other stay on track toward your individual goals. Both of you have a chance to walk about recent wins, review current challenges and come up with strategies to implement before your next conversation.

To get started, here is a five-step action plan.

Step 1: Search for the right person.

You can find an accountabuddy online or in person. Your search would be similar to the way you would look for a virtual or local community. Go to local meetups, join topic-related forums, talk to members of your online groups and reach out to friends who are interested in this type of partnership.

Once you've found a few groups, spend time getting to know the members. The purpose is to find *one person*, not dozens of people. In a way, you should treat your search is if you are looking for a date—find someone who seems interesting, schedule a time to have an initial conversation and then see if you click. This is an ongoing process, so expect to spend at least a week or two searching for the right person.

Step 2: Be open to someone with a different background.

Your buddy shouldn't be your exact clone. In fact, you should look for a person who has a similar level of success, but also has strengths and weaknesses that differ from yours.

For instance, Tom (my accountabuddy) is a writer who has achieved success by creating a paid blog service that has scaled into a business that specializes in creating content for WordPress sites.

We both use writing as our primary way to generate revenue, yet our business models are completely different. That means we each bring a unique perspective to the relationship. We use our perspectives to ping ideas off one another and suggest ideas the other person might not have considered.

To find the *right* accountabuddy, I recommend looking for someone who is at (or slightly above) your current level of success. You want to challenge one another, *not* create an arrangement where one person is coaching the other. I have been on both sides of this situation, and the relationship always fails because one person feels like they're not getting value for their time.

Step 3: Approach your favorite candidate.

When you find someone who seems like an ideal accountabuddy, ask if s/he is interested in this type of meeting. Explain the concept, outline the mutual benefits of the commitment and simply ask if she is interested.

If either one of you is uncomfortable jumping right into "accountabuddy status," have an initial conversation and then make a decision after you've had a chance to get to know each other.

Step 4: Pick a day, time and type of meeting.

An accountabuddy meeting can be structured in a variety of ways. Some people meet in person, on the phone or via Skype, while others send updates through email, text or social media networks. The platform doesn't matter as long as you regularly check in with each other and provide *mutual* accountability.

Furthermore, it's important to keep a consistent schedule. The two of you should sit down, compare your weekly schedules and find a day/time that works best on a consistent basis. Sure, there will be times when you have to switch up the meeting time, but it's important to schedule a time block that becomes a permanent part of your week. When you regularly meet at the same time, your subconscious mind will start to come up with ideas and topics to discuss during your next meeting.

Step 5: Create weekly accountability statements.

You want to make what are known as *accountability statements*. These are action items you promise to complete before the next meeting. In a way, they're similar to milestones because they're small actions that are part of a larger goal.

The best type of accountability statement is one that is related to your primary goal, has a clear outcome and is *doable* in a specific time frame.

To make the process easy to remember, I suggest using the PACT acronym:

- **P.** Possible
- **A.** Actionable
- **C.** Clear
- **T.** Time-Bound Deadline

Let's take a closer look at each element:

P: Possible:

Is the goal in the accountability statement achievable?

While it's okay to aim high and fall short from time to time, your goal should be something realistic that you can complete in the allotted timeframe. If you are trying to write a book, for example, a statement of "I will write 5,000 words during the next week" is an achievable goal if you already average 1,000 words per day.

A: Actionable

Can you take action on the goal?

You might be surprised to learn that many people try to set goals they have little control over.

For instance, "I will get more people to like me" is not an achievable goal because it doesn't have a clear set of actions attached. It doesn't say *how* you will achieve the goal.

This is a far better statement: "I will say five nice things to five different people every day for the next week." More people might like you as a result of your efforts, but you have complete control over the outcome. You either reach your goal or you don't.

C: Clear

Your accountability statement should be clear and without equivocation. It shouldn't include a series of exceptions or reasons you can't achieve the goal. The statement should always be as simple and direct as possible.

For instance, it is "I will write 5,000 words this week," **not** "I will write 5,000 words this week unless I get super busy or have to answer a bunch of emails."

When forming accountability statements, you should always consider potential obstacles and have a plan for dealing with them. Adjust your accountability statements according to what you think might prevent you from succeeding. If you know the upcoming week will be filled with personal obligations, all you have to do is adjust your milestone accordingly. "I will write 3,000 words this week" is a good example.

T: Time-Bound

There should be a clear deadline for your commitment. In most cases, the deadline will be the date of your next meeting. However, if you both realize there will be a lengthy break before your next session, then go ahead and create a deadline. Agree to email or text each other with the results.

When you follow these five steps, you'll get maximum value from an accountabuddy meeting. Just remember to focus on the challenges you're both facing, provide honest feedback to the other person and create accountability statements that use the PACT formula. Do these things on a continuous basis and you can easily break a major goal into a series of doable tasks.

Throughout this section, I compared an accountabuddy to a mastermind group, which is a regular meeting where you connect with a *group of people* instead of one individual. There are many benefits to using this strategy, but there are also a few drawbacks. Let's talk about mastermind groups and how they can become an important part of your accountability.

Accountability Strategy #4

Forming a Mastermind Group

The concept of the mastermind group was popularized by Napoleon Hill in his book *Think and Grow Rich*. Hill didn't "create" this idea, but he was one of the first people to present it to the masses as a valuable way to build alliances with others who share mutual interests.

The word *mastermind* describes the synergy created when several people come together to combine their efforts toward a common goal. The idea here is that the total effort (in terms of mental power) equals more than the sum of its parts.

We can see examples of masterminding throughout history, although it may not have been identified by the same term. A great example is the Committee of Five of the Second Continental Congress. Committee members wrote the Declaration of Independence, a powerful document that shaped a nation. That's masterminding in the truest sense of the word.

Here are some other examples of famous mastermind groups:

Algonquin Round Table: A celebrated group of New York City writers, critics, actors and wits. Members met for lunch each day at the Algonquin Hotel from 1919 until roughly 1929. At these luncheons, they engaged in wisecracks, wordplay and witticisms that, through the newspaper columns of Round Table members, were disseminated across the country. In its ten years of association, the Round Table and a number of its members acquired national reputations, both for their contributions to literature and for their sparkling wit.

The Junto: A club for mutual improvement established in 1727 by Benjamin Franklin in Philadelphia. Also known as the *Leather Apron Club*, its purpose was to debate questions of morals, politics and natural philosophy, and to exchange knowledge of business affairs. Members of the Junto created a subscription library of their own books.

The Vagabonds: Between 1915 and 1924, Henry Ford, Thomas Edison, Harvey Firestone and John Burroughs, calling themselves the Four Vagabonds, embarked on a series of summer camping trips. The idea was initiated in 1914 when Ford and Burroughs visited Edison in Florida and toured the Everglades. The notion blossomed the next year when Ford, Edison and Firestone were in California for the Panama-Pacific Exposition. They visited Luther Burbank and then drove from Riverside to San Diego.

In modern times, we see masterminding at work in areas such as organized religion, politics, education and the military. As you can see, the concept has expanded significantly since its inception in the business world.

The primary benefit of masterminding is stimulating new ideas, getting motivation from other members and providing inspiration to others as you move forward to meet your goals.

Before we dive into the process of finding (or forming) a mastermind group, let's go over the advantages and disadvantages of this concept.

Advantages:

- *Accountability*: Having a set group of people to whom you can turn for ideas and support is invaluable. Think of it this way—if *one* accountabuddy is good, imagine how much you can learn from an entire group. When you have three to five people in a close-knit group, there will always be someone available to take your call or meet with you if you desperately need advice.

- *Feedback*: Being able to meet with your mastermind group for feedback is like having multiple coaches. You can sit around a table (or a bar, or a computer if you use Skype) to hear what each person in the group thinks about your situation. Members may have different perspectives and think of new approaches you had not considered. You don't always have to go with their suggestions, but sometimes you'll find that your next "ah-ha moment" comes from a casual comment made by another group member.

- *Collaborative intelligence*: Multiple inputs and viewpoints are far better than a single one. Your mastermind group members can pool their intelligence to offer a crowdsourced solution to any obstacle. *Have a problem you can't seem to solve?* Ask your mastermind group and watch them come together to offer solutions you can use.

- *Expanded networks*: The people in your group will have connections you might never have on your own. If you need to get in touch with someone who previously seemed unreachable, one member of your group might be able to offer an introduction.

- *Ability to learn new things*: Each member should have a slightly different set of skills and knowledge. Meeting with a diverse group of people makes it easier to learn, grow and adapt new strategies. However, members shouldn't be so diverse that there's no crossover or common ground to which you all can relate.

For example, a nonfiction writer, fiction writer, publisher and blogger would make a good mastermind group because they all have a business that revolves around creating content for a specific audience.

On the flip side, a writer, artist, fitness expert and businessman might not share enough common experiences to give value to one another.

Cross promotion: If members of your mastermind are in similar (but non-competing) businesses, you can cross-promote each other's products or services. This type of networking allows group members to reach people they would not be able to reach alone.

Disadvantages:

- It can be easy to fall into a group that's a waste of time if you don't carefully select the group members. If you're an energetic action taker, it can be frustrating to surround yourself with people who have a casual approach to life and business.
- You may find that you have one or two group members who monopolize everyone's time when you meet as a group. Every member should be given the same amount of time and attention to share their experiences.
- When there are too many weak links in the group, the meeting will quickly become a therapy session instead of an action-focused conversation that helps all the members.
- If you find you are stuck in the wrong group, it can be difficult to leave the group without hurting feelings and burning bridges.
- You may find that you give more than you receive in a group that isn't well-matched or balanced.

While a mastermind group has *some* disadvantages, it's easy to prevent them if you're careful about the selection process. My advice is to take steps similar to the ones you would take to find an accountabuddy.

Not only should you look for the right people, you must make sure it's the right *mix* of people. In the next section, I'll go through a six-step process for building a mastermind group that's focused on getting results for *each* member.

6 Steps for Creating a Powerful Mastermind Group

As we've discussed, picking (or forming) the *wrong* mastermind group can quickly become a massive waste of your time. Even worse—surrounding yourself with people who have conflicting mindsets can often lead to a de-motivated attitude or lack of desire to work on your goals. That's why it's important to be very selective with the people you ask to be part of the group. Here is the six-step process I recommend.

Step #1: Find the right people for your mastermind group.

Meeting with like-minded people on a regular basis is the key to tapping into the power of masterminding. You will need to find peers who share similar goals but are also different enough that you can provide feedback based on a unique perspective. This will add diversity and value to your mastermind group.

The best way to get started is to create a list of people in your personal network. Your list should include people you already know, friends of friends or people you *want* to know.

To create the optimal group, you should look for the following characteristics in potential members:

- Similar experience levels
- Ambition and a strong desire for success

- Good values and beliefs
- No direct competitors—the last thing you want to do is give away a trade secret to someone who has the ability to gain a competitive advantage.
- Local (if group meetings are local and not virtual)
- Now that we know the qualities a potential mastermind group member should have, here's where to look for members:
- People you know
- People who know people you know
- People in related fields you would like to know better
- People you respect
- Connections of friends, family members or colleagues
- Facebook groups based on a similar interest
- Meetup.com
- LinkedIn.com
- Forums, blogs and websites related to your field
- Want ads
- Social media profiles
- Your own blog posts

You've probably heard about the theory of six degrees of separation (or at least you know about the game called "Six Degrees of Kevin Bacon"). The point here is it's surprisingly easy to connect to virtually anyone if you know how to leverage your existing personal networks. Look at the social media profiles of your friends and acquaintances. Browse their networks and write down the names of people who stand out. Ask your mutual contacts what they know about each person. Keep working your personal connections until someone introduces you to a person who might be a good match for your mastermind group.

After the initial introduction, schedule a phone conversation and take time to get to know the potential group member. If you feel there is a high level of rapport, see if s/he is interested in joining a mastermind group.

Step #2: Make a mastermind proposal.

How do you pitch a mastermind group to a potential member? Here are a few strategies you should follow:

1) Build rapport. Asking someone to join a mastermind group is a significant request. Time is one of our most precious assets, so most success-minded people won't join a mastermind unless they know the person asking and feel the meeting will be a valuable use of their time.

Most people won't make such a commitment unless they have at least a casual relationship with the person doing the asking. Don't just dive in and ask strangers to join your group. Get to know them, talk a few times on the phone, see if you get along and then propose the idea of being part of a mastermind.

2) Show proven results: Few people will want to be part of a group unless one (or all) of the members has achieved a high degree of success. In other words, you might want to hold off on forming one until you can prove that you're passionate about your goal and have something of value to offer other members.

3) Have a clear purpose: Is it a professional or personal mastermind? What are your main areas of focus? What type of background is required to join?

Prospective members will want to know specifics to see if they will get any value from the group. Remember—most people are willing to help others, but they also want to see clear evidence that joining the mastermind will benefit them in some way.

4) Detail the commitment required: For a mastermind to work, members must be willing to commit to a specific amount of time on a regular basis. They also need to show up and stay for the entire meeting. Be open and up front about these obligations from the beginning, and you can weed out those who aren't that interested.

5) Provide plenty of detail: Be clear on the details of the meetings. (I'll go over specifics in the next steps.)

6) Invite potential members: Select a group of people you think will work well together, and then invite them to join. A few might not be completely sure about the idea, so you might want to suggest a "trial" month and emphasize that they can make a decision at the end.

It's not hard to find potential members of a mastermind group. The trick is to make sure everyone meshes well with one another. You need to look for people who work hard to reach their *goals and* have a positive attitude about life in general.

Step #3: Decide when and where to meet.

What you decide for this step will depend greatly on the nature of the group. If your goal is to create a virtual mastermind group with people from all over the world, then you will be limited to voice over IP (VoIP) options like the following:

- Skype
- FaceTime
- Google Hangouts

If you're organizing a local group, on the other hand, then your options include anything from a casual meetup at Panera Bread all the way to reserving a business conference room for an entire weekend.

If you plan to meet over dinner or coffee, be sure to pick a spot that is quiet or has a private area for your meeting. You need to be able to talk without being overheard by other diners or forced to talk over loud restaurant noise.

Another option to consider is meeting at a member's home. You could even rotate host duties so everyone shares a little of the responsibility. Obviously, this really depends on your comfort level with other members of the mastermind. If you aren't sure about your group yet, meet in a public place until you are comfortable enough to have a meeting in a member's home.

Whether you decide to meet in person or virtually, it is important to make sure every meeting has minimal distractions and all members are fully present in the conversation.

Step #4: Create rules for the mastermind group.

A mastermind group requires a formal set of rules that gives structure to the meetings. Implementing rules prevents one person from monopolizing all the time, ensures all conversations focus on specific goals and provides opportunities for members to receive honest feedback on their challenges.

With that in mind, there are few things to consider when creating group rules:

- Define the goal(s) for the mastermind group. Group goals are similar to a company's mission statement—they create a solid foundation for the group and help group members understand what they should expect at every meeting.

  During your first session, ask each person what they hope to get out of the group and how everyone can help them. It's equally important to cover what members *don't want* from a group. This last question is extremely important because some people enjoy an atmosphere of friendly banter, while others prefer a strictly business approach. It's best to start by identifying any potential landmines and dealing with them immediately.

- After the first meeting, draft a written list of ground rules for the group. Each member should have an opportunity to add to, delete or edit these rules, so the final version will be a blend of everyone's expectations. (You can use a program like Google Docs to share this file and anything else you create as a group.)

  Keep these rules on hand during each meeting. You should also consider reading the ground rules aloud before the first couple of meetings to keep make sure everyone is aware of the group's expectations.

- In all meetings, stress how important it is to respect the time of others. Keep everyone focused by creating an agenda for each meeting. You should create an outline of discussion topics and agree to limit the amount of time spent on each topic. Make sure each person is able to view the outline to keep the meeting moving and on track.
- Give each person a time limit to talk about a particular topic. The time limit should be the same for all members. A good rule of thumb is five to 15 minutes per person.
- Limit the amount of time people are given to respond to comments made by other members. Having a time constraint in place gives the meeting structure, keeps things moving forward and helps make the best use of everyone's time.
- Set up a guideline that says any discussion should focus on accountability-related topics. It's okay to engage in fun banter, but you don't want the meetings to turn into a free-for-all where people waste time joking around or complaining about their businesses.
- Establish guidelines for how decisions will be made within the group, such as how the group functions, when the group will meet and what actions the group will take.
- Create systems for getting rid of noncompliant members and finding replacements for members who leave the group. Again, all members will be involved in setting up these guidelines, which will promote unity and make it easier to keep the group what you want it to be.
- Clarify that the group is not a place for egos and competition. All group members should work together and respect each other for the mastermind to work as desired.

If you enjoy having a lot of personal freedom, then following a long list of rules might seem too restrictive. That said, having this structure keeps everyone focused on talking about their goals and providing actionable advice to one another. Fortunately, if you're smart about finding the right people, these rules won't need to be enforced because each member will understand the importance of making sure the conversation stays on topic.

Step #5: Maintain supporting documents.

In addition to maintaining a set of rules, you should also create documents that provide structure for the meetings. (Again, Google Docs a great tool for this.) These files don't have to be fancy; you just need a simple document covering each of the following items:

- The group's statement of purpose.
- The guidelines for introducing new topics, speaking, responding, and joining and leaving the group.
- A statement of procedure outlining what to do if there is a conflict or someone is unwilling to adhere to the guidelines.
- An outline of each meeting with a list of discussion topics and a time limit for each one.
- Dates and times for future meetings.
- A member list with contact information, including email address, phone number, time zone, website address and social media information for each member.
- A document for members to suggest topics for discussion or ideas to make the meetings more effective.
- Meeting minutes for everyone to review, especially members who missed a meeting. You can create audio or video recordings of each meeting, or have someone in the group act as secretary.

You don't have to maintain every file I just mentioned, but if you start the group in an organized fashion, it will be easier to convince members to treat each session as a valuable use of their time.

Step #6: Create "hot seat" time (optional).

The "hot seat" is a powerful concept I use with my mastermind group. During a hot seat, members get extra time to talk about their goals, but everyone has to focus on the challenges they're experiencing. A person's time in the hot seat can last anywhere from 15 to 30 minutes, but even a short session is extremely useful because other members provide feedback and present the person in the hot seat with a series of ideas that can be implemented immediately.

The hot seat should have a rotating schedule so everyone has a chance to benefit from it. This means Member A will be the focal point during the first meeting; then Member B will have her time during the second meeting. Follow this schedule until everyone has an opportunity to be on the hot seat. At the *next* meeting, start the rotation all over again with Member A.

As you can see, it's not that hard to form a powerful mastermind group. That said, you might find that some of the components are a little confusing. That's why I provide a sample group structure in the next section.

How to Structure a Mastermind Meeting

Remember—the *true purpose* of a mastermind is to help members achieve their goals. With that in mind, the meetings need to be structured in a way that limits the amount of time each member has to speak.

We've already covered the systems you need to put into place to form the foundation of the group, but let's take a look at some of the nuts and bolts of running an effective meeting.

- **Keep precise meeting times.** Schedule your meetings on consistent days and at consistent times so people get used to attending on a certain day—like every first and third Wednesday at 7 p.m. The date and time is up to you, but the important thing is consistency.

- All members need to be punctual, with a five-minute buffer for people who are running a *little late* (like someone having a Wi-Fi connectivity issue for a virtual group).

- We all have busy lives, so respect everyone's time by keeping a tight schedule and not allowing the "chronically late" arrivals to derail these meetings. If you have someone like this in the group, then perhaps it's best to pick a different person.

- **Stick to the agenda and meeting structure.** When people start talking, it's easy to go down the rabbit hole of a new topic. If you stick to the agenda, however, the meeting will be productive and meet the objectives of all group members. Print out an agenda and have it in front of everyone at the meeting, or send it in a text or email. Have members follow along with the agenda during the meeting so everyone stays on track.

- **Keep "talking time" equal for all members.** I know we have touched on this, but it is worth repeating. If you need to use a timer, then use it for everyone! If you have a large group, you may need to limit speaking time to five minutes per person. Small groups with only a handful of members may be able to increase the limit to 10 or 15 minutes. In any case, you need to stick to the limit and make a rule stating that no interruptions are allowed (other than questions and suggestions) while someone has the "floor." You can also make a rule stating that no one can provide feedback until after a person has finished speaking.

- **Determine whether or not you need one or more group facilitators.** For a smaller group, you only need one facilitator. If you have a group with 10 or more members, two facilitators would be better. You may even find you don't really need a facilitator because everyone does a great job sticking to the rules. When you first start a mastermind group, it's good to have a facilitator to give each meeting structure, keep people focused and make sure the conversation is flowing.

- **Begin each meeting with an overview**. Each member should have 30 seconds to one minute to update the group on struggles and/or successes since the last meeting. In most cases, the update should relate to any accountability statements members made the week before.

- **Set aside hot-seat time**. The hot seat provides members with an individualized level of attention and honest feedback about what they can do next. Being in the spotlight can be stressful, but it can also provide amazing insight into strategies members hadn't yet considered.

- **End each meeting with a wrap-up.** During this time, the facilitator can wrap up loose ends and provide an opportunity for members to share quick items, ask questions or suggest agenda topics for the following meeting. Lastly, the meeting should end with each member sharing an accountability statement they promise to accomplish before the next meeting.

If you want to run a well-organized mastermind meeting, you need to be able to manage your time effectively. To illustrate this point, here is the format we use in my mastermind group:

- There are five members, each with a different type of online business.
- Each meeting is at 2 p.m. (EST) every other Wednesday and lasts for one hour.
- We begin with five to 10 minutes of bantering and catching up.
- Each member spends five minutes talking about their wins from the past two weeks.
- One member gets 20 minutes of hot-seat time to talk about current business challenges.
- We end the meeting with a single, "big win" accountability statement we promise to complete before the next meeting.

Doesn't look too hard, right?

Joining a mastermind group can be an effective strategy for overcoming the challenges you face on a regular basis. However, it's not a magic pill for every obstacle. Sometimes you'll find there are certain situations where you need the guidance of an expert who specializes in a particular area. That's when you might want to consider hiring a coach, which we'll cover in the next section.

Accountability Strategy #5

Working with a Coach

W hy does every sport have a coach? Because coaching often leads to a substantial improvement in the performance of athletes. Not only do coaches keep players motivated, they also create an accountability environment that forces everyone to stick to the primary goal of every team—winning.

The word "coach" itself is a catchall that includes two types of assistance:

1) There are coaches who *aren't* subject-matter experts. For instance, a head football coach knows how to run the team as a cohesive unit, but isn't an expert on each position (like the quarterback). His job is to understand the big picture and to guide players toward winning the game.

2) There are coaches who *are* subject-matter experts. For instance, business consultants often have specific areas of expertise. They have experienced a variety of situations throughout their careers, so they can provide top-notch information based on these experiences.

A coach's level of skill and experience varies from person to person. What you want is to work with someone who has mastered a specific skill related to one of your goals.

For instance, you could hire a coach to help with public speaking, an online business or losing weight. Just think back to the section where we talked about the different types of accountability. Odds are, you can find a coach that specializes in these areas.

Is a Coach Right for You?

Before you decide to hire a coach, it's important to know what you are looking for and how this person can help. I recommend answering a few questions before you start searching for a coach:

- Do I need a coach to help me uncover things about myself or discover who I am and what I want to do in life?
- Do I need a coach to be a consultant or come in and give me a direct and specific path to reaching my goals?
- Do I need a coach to be a counselor who answers questions, diagnoses problems and sets me on a path to recovery?
- Do I need motivation from this coach, or do I simply need a strategy to follow?

Working with a coach can be the secret to mastering a specific skill, but it could also cost you precious time (and money). To fully understand what's required, I recommend understanding both the advantages and disadvantages of this strategy.

Advantages:

- You get one-on-one assistance and guidance.
- The services are highly tailored to your needs and focused on your specific goals.
- You can benefit from the coach's experience.
- You may be able to find a mentor who will serve as your coach, which means you might get these services for free. Some mentors don't ask for payment, so you can reap the rewards without opening your wallet.
- A coach may have professional contacts you can use to grow and expand your personal network.

Disadvantages:

- Most coaches treat their services like a job, so there *will* be a payment involved.
- Extensive coaching can get expensive, especially if you want to work with a true subject-matter expert. The cost can be as high as a few hundred dollars per hour.
- There can be a clash of personalities if you don't find the right coach.

Making the decision to work with a coach should be done with a lot of planning and careful consideration. Make sure this person can *actually* provide assistance in the area where you need help. You shouldn't treat the coaching decision like a one-size-fits-all arrangement.

For instance, if you need help with public speaking *and* with running a business, then it makes sense to hire a coach for each of these areas.

The hard part is knowing when someone is actually qualified to coach you. That's why, in the next section, I go over a few qualities a good coach should have.

12 Qualities of a Good Coach

What characteristics separate the great from the not-so-good coaches?

Honestly, the answer will vary because we all have our own personal preferences. You might prefer a strict, no-nonsense personality, while someone else likes working with a coach who gives informal, "follow-your-heart" advice.

Just remember that you are spending your hard-earned money to work with a coach, so it's important find one who demonstrates the qualities you need to master a specific goal.

It's been my experience that a great coach will:

1) Have a proven track record of success related to your goal.
2) Provide an organized action plan for overcoming a challenge.
3) Be balanced with feedback, giving positive comments just as often as the negative ones.
4) Have solid communication skills and the ability to give you advice while listening to your feedback.
5) Be available throughout the week if you have a quick question.
6) Understand your broad vision, but also be able to focus on the little details.
7) Monitor and track your progress with metrics and milestones.

8) Set realistic goals you can achieve on a consistent basis.
9) Analyze the issues you face and present you with ideas you haven't considered.
10) Challenge you if s/he feels you are slacking off on your efforts. (A coach should be tough and demanding when the situation warrants it.)
11) Focus on their own growth—often hiring their own coach.
12) Force you to be accountable on a weekly basis by requiring you to take specific actions before your next meeting.

You might require additional qualities beyond the 12 I just listed. If so, be sure to write them down before talking to a potential coach.

In addition to looking for certain characteristics, you should also take the time to interview a coach before you start working together. In the next section, we'll go over a few questions to ask before making a hiring decision.

Questions to Ask a Potential Coach

Hiring a coach should be a thorough process in which you research possible candidates, ask for referrals from your network and conduct interviews with the best candidates. In a way, it's like hiring an employee, but the only difference is this person will end up telling you what to do on a weekly basis.

The hiring process is an important step because it gives you a chance to learn about a coach's philosophy and style *before* you pay for their service. That's why I recommend asking some (or all) of the following questions:

What is your work experience or experience with this goal?

A coach doesn't necessarily need to be a subject-matter expert, but the person you choose should have a passing familiarity with your goal.

While career experience in this area is helpful, you should also consider working with someone who is self-taught and gained experience from the "school of hard knocks." Personally, I'd much rather work with a coach who spends his or her time actually *doing* a task than one who gained expertise from the comfort of a secure job.

How long have you been coaching? How many clients have you had?

Like any craft, a little bit of experience and practice go a long way. Just like you wouldn't want to be the first patient of a new brain surgeon, you probably don't want to be the first client of a coach with a new practice.

Where (or how) were you trained?

Once upon a time, all it took to sell your services as a coach was hanging a shingle and calling yourself a "coach." That is no longer true. There are many professional coach training paths, certifications, qualifications and professional organizations. As with any other professional you hire, you want to ensure that your coach is qualified and trained by a reputable organization.

The International Coach Federation (ICF) is one of the most respected organizations. The ICF sets standards for career and life coaches. You will also want to investigate the level of training your coach has received. There are three different levels of ICF-approved training:

1) Associate Certified Coach (ACC)
2) Professional Certified Coach (PCC)
3) Master Certified Coach (MCC).

Be careful when choosing a coach based on certifications, however. You don't want a coach who focuses on certificates and accolades to the detriment of everything else. This goes back to my comment about the *school of hard knocks*. If you have a coach who actually spends time *doing* the task you need to master, you're likely to receive much better advice than you would if you hired someone based on certifications and awards alone.

What is your approach to coaching?

There isn't a "right" coaching style because everyone has their own tastes and preferences. You should talk with each coach at length about your needs and look for someone whose style matches what you need to achieve your goals.

This is an important step in finding someone who is compatible with what you need.

How do you meet with clients?

Do they have an office? Do they meet up at the local Starbucks? Do they connect with clients online? By phone?

Again, there isn't a right answer here, but you should know what you want ahead of time and hire someone based on your preferences.

Can you describe a coaching session from start to finish?

The coach should be able to articulate how a normal session is structured. Even better—some coaches offer a free introductory session for you to evaluate their services before you make a commitment. If you find someone who offers this option, I recommend you try it out.

How do they measure coaching success?

I am a big fan of metrics, so I feel this is an important consideration. You should look for a coach who uses measurements and metrics to track your success toward a major goal. Not only will this help you stay on track, it also demonstrates the overall effectiveness of the coach's service.

Describe a major obstacle encountered by a client and tell me how you helped him/her through it.

Quality coaching skills are demonstrated *not* when everything goes perfectly, but when something goes wrong. Coaches should be able to explain how clients benefit from their services. Ask a coach to summarize a client challenge and explain how his or her advice helped overcome that challenge.

What results can I expect after 10 sessions?

A coach can't promise immediate results because it takes time to achieve major goals. However, there should be some indication of what results you'll receive if you stick with their program for the next few months.

How much do you charge for a session?

A coaching session can vary greatly in price from one coach to another—anywhere from $50 per hour all the way up to $1,000 per day.

What type of contract do you use?

Contracts are common with coaches. The contract should describe the number of sessions, length of each session and the amount of time for each meeting. Coaching contracts should also lay out a cancellation policy and specify who is responsible for making contact if the sessions are by phone.

Be sure to carefully read over this contract, closely examine each section and ask for additional clarification if you're confused about any clause. It's better to ask questions *before* signing your name.

Now that you know how to pre-screen a coach, let's talk about where you can find a true expert to help you improve a particular skill or reach a big goal.

How to Get Started with a Coach

While there are hundreds of ways to find a coach, you want to look for someone who has the background and expertise to help you get measurable results. My recommendation is to start with your personal network and talk to people who achieved success with a similar goal. Perhaps *they're* willing to coach you or know someone who can. If someone gives you a coach's name, ask *why* they endorse this person.

There are also a number of online resources that can connect you with a coach. (Just remember to ask the interview questions I listed *before* signing any long-term contract). Here are some resources you might want to try:

- Coach.me: Not only does this app allow you to track habits, it also has a marketplace where you can get online coaching at a low cost. While the coaching is not as in-depth as a live one-on-one call, it's a good service if you have a limited budget. Often, a weekly check-in is all you'll need to stick to a goal.

- Coach.me also offers free community support via an online forum and Q & A section, so if you really don't have the budget, you can get help without spending a dollar. But keep in mind that you often get what you pay for. It has been said that *the most expensive advice is free advice*, because you never know if the person is an actual expert on the topic.

- Clarity.fm: This site connects entrepreneurs with top industry experts who help with market research, give strategic advice and teach people how to master specialized business skills. It's a pay-per-call service. You let them know what your topic or question is, and they find you an expert and schedule the call so you can get the support and accountability you need.
- The benefit of Clarity.fm is you're billed on a per-minute basis, so you won't need to pay for an hour-long call if you only need answers to a few questions.
- Finally, Clarity.fm is an excellent place to test different coaches and hire the best one on a full-time basis. My advice is to pay for an introductory call with three or four potential coaches, talk with each for 30 minutes and then hire the person who provides the most insight during your meeting. You can usually tell within the first five minutes whether or not a person can provide actionable advice.
- Accomplishment Coaching: This site lets you search for coaches by specific criteria: education, experience and area of focus. This makes it easy to find the right coach to meet your needs. The Accomplishment Coaching website has a powerful quote: *"Who exactly seeks out coaching? Winners who want even more out of life!"*
- Life Coach: This site offers different levels of personal coaching and support based on your budget constraints. It features a user-friendly search option so you can find the type of coaching you need—like online coaching *or* phone coaching.
- **Personal and Life Coaching Websites**: This may seem overly simple, but it's easy to find a long list of qualified coaches by doing a Google search for terms such as "personal coaching" or "life coaching." The coaches found online usually offer a wide range of services, from a short phone call to get you started all the way up to weekly coaching calls.

You can also search for a coach based on specific goals. Use terms like *writing coach, business coach* or *relationship coach* to find the right person. See too many results? Add a modifier related to your geographic area, such as *writing coach New York* or *relationship coach San Francisco.* Coaching is a big industry, so if you're willing to do your research, it's not hard to a qualified person who specializes in helping people achieve a specific goal.

Coaching is an excellent strategy for adding accountability to your life, but it can also be expensive. If you lack the funds needed to hire a coach, then perhaps you can get similar support by working with an accountabuddy or connecting with people via a mobile app. You might even be able to work with a mentor who is willing to share their wisdom for free. In the next section, we'll go over the strategy for finding someone like this.

Accountability Strategy #6

Meeting with a Mentor

On the surface, mentorship might *seem* like a type of coaching. It usually involves an experienced expert guiding a young (but eager) individual. If you look closely, though, the mentor-mentee relationship is often deeper than the relationship between a coach and a client. That's because mentors only work with a handful of mentees and focus on passing along <u>everything</u> they've learned in a lifetime.

There are many examples of powerful mentor-mentee relationships throughout history. It's not unusual for a successful mentee to start mentoring a younger person at some point. This is a great way to pay it forward and make an impact on the future.

For instance, Andrew Carnegie was mentored by Thomas A. Scott. In turn, Napoleon Hill was mentored by Andrew Carnegie. With his book, *Think and Grow Rich*, Napoleon Hill mentored an entire generation of people interested in self-improvement.

A mentor is also similar to an accountabuddy because you will get accountability and support. The difference is that the mentor-mentee relationship is more one-sided than the relationship between two accountabuddies.

Mentors make ideal accountability partners because they keep you focused on personal-development goals. These are just some of the ways a mentor can help you:

- Providing insider tips about how an industry *really* works

- Giving advice based on years of experience
- Listing alternatives you may not have considered
- Identifying career blind spots you might not see
- Educating you on important disciplines and skills to develop
- Providing ongoing guidance to help you reach your fullest potential

When seeking a mentor, you need to find someone who understands what you are trying to do and has years of experience related to your goal. You will talk with your mentor from time to time, but not necessarily on a schedule like you would have with a coach. A mentor will guide you and provide advice, but they usually don't involve themselves directly in the day-to-day aspects of meeting your goals. It's more of a "big-picture" relationship.

Now, a mentor isn't always your best solution for accountability. There are times when a paid coach is a better option. Consider a few points outlined on the Management Mentors website:

Coaching is task oriented, while mentoring is relationship oriented.

Coaches focus on concrete issues, such as more effective management, following a better diet or developing specific skills. This is why a coach needs to be a content expert.

Mentoring is focused on the relationship, providing a safe environment where you can share the issues affecting you as you work to meet your goals. A mentor will also help you work on things like achieving work-life balance, building self-confidence and having the right mindset to be successful.

Coaching is short-term, while mentoring is long-term.

Typically, a coaching relationship is one that lasts a few weeks or a few months as you work toward your goals. There is usually a beginning and end to the time spent together—and the time frame depends on your goals or needs.

A mentor is someone who supports you for the long haul. Because you are building a true relationship, you spend time getting to know one other, which builds a foundation of trust and respect. You should expect this relationship to last years, even decades.

Coaching is focused on performance, while mentoring is focused on personal development.

With a coach, you work on specific issues related to your short-term goals. You may be fine-tuning current skills or learning something new. Once you have mastered those skills, you may no longer need the coach to guide you.

With a mentor, you will be working on a deeper, more personal level of development. You will address issues that will impact your life and your future beyond the goals you are striving to reach.

Coaching can begin immediately, without a lot of preparation, while mentoring requires more forethought and planning.

When you work with a coach who already has a particular set of skills, you are able to start working on your goals right away. An experienced coach knows which skills are needed to get to the next level.

With mentoring, there is an adjustment period. Such a period is necessary for identifying the focus of the relationship and allowing the mentor to learn more about who you are and what you'd like to achieve.

Still not sure if a mentor is right for you? Then consider the following advantages and disadvantages of this form of accountability.

Advantages:

- A mentor offers a combination of life experience and caring guidance.
- A mentor serves as an accountability partner, but you receive most of the guidance and support.

- The right mentor can help you identify personal issues you may not recognize on your own.
- A good mentor inspires you to be the best you can be in all areas of your life.
- A skilled mentor serves as a sounding board and gives you opportunities to discuss the challenges you are facing.
- A great mentor asks the hard questions so you can work on deeper issues.
- A skilled mentor sees your potential and encourages greatness in you.

Disadvantages:
- It's not always easy to find a good mentor.
- If you don't set boundaries, there might be issues with maintaining a strict mentor-mentee relationship.
- There can be a clash of personalities if the mentor isn't right for you.
- It can be challenging to know when the mentorship has run its course.
- If structure for the mentorship is not set in advance, it can become too much like a friendship.

Working with a mentor can have an amazing impact on your personal development. It's great to know someone is there to cheer your successes and give you a kick in the butt when you're slacking off. If this sounds like a relationship you would like to pursue, then check out the next chapter, where I detail an eight-step process for working with a mentor.

8 Steps for Working with a Mentor

I'll be honest here...it's not easy to find a mentor.

And *even* if you identify the right person, s/he might be too busy to lend support on a regular basis.

The process of finding a mentor is often like trying to find a needle in a haystack.

If you're serious about finding a mentor, then you need a game plan for not only locating the perfect person, but also convincing them to provide mentoring on a continuous basis.

To make this happen, I recommend the following eight-step process.

Step #1. Decide what you need from a mentor.

Mentors can assist with any goal, so it's important to start with the areas where you need the most help. Set aside a few hours one day to write down your problems, any obstacles you are facing and goals you want to achieve in life.

Once you complete this list, think about the *type* of mentor that can help you. What are the qualities you'd need from this person? Is he or she passionate or laid back? Outspoken or reserved? Results driven or flexible with your goals?

Success doesn't require a specific type of personality. Instead, a mentor's personality should match what you need so you can take advantage of your natural strengths.

Finally, create a "wish list" to identify the characteristics of a perfect mentor and use it whenever you encounter someone who might be able to help.

#2. Pick a type of mentor.

Just like there are many types of coaches, there are many types of mentors. You should work with one who has experience with a specific goal. For instance, you could look for mentors in the following areas:

- **Education:** Professors, older students with more experience
- **Business:** Acquaintances with a lot of experience, your old boss (your current boss shouldn't be a mentor due to a potential conflict of interest) or respected coworkers
- **Sports:** Coaches, trainers, veteran players or retired players
- **Health/weight loss:** Acquaintances who have mastered a healthy lifestyle or maintained a consistent weight loss
- **Lifestyle:** Acquaintances who have lived life to the fullest, gone through some of the issues you are facing or achieved the goals you want to achieve

#3. Identify the help you need from a mentor.

Ask the following questions to determine how much help you'd require from a mentor:

- What would you like to learn?
- What are you looking for from your mentor?
- How often would you like to meet?
- Where will you connect—email, phone, or in person?

#4. Make a list of potential candidates.

Write down a list of possibilities, including people you know well and those you admire from a distance. Shoot for the stars with this list! Many famous and successful people have personal assistants that they mentor and train. It isn't outside the realm of possibility to get a job working for someone successful and end up in a mentoring relationship.

Keep in mind that, when you aim really high, you may get turned down a lot. However, all your effort will pay off when you finally find someone willing to share their knowledge and expertise.

#5. Map out an approach for contacting potential mentors.

Going up to someone and asking them to be your mentor, unless you know them well, is a bit like asking a stranger to marry you. It can be too much all at once, and you run the risk of being rejected during your very first interaction.

You need to build a relationship with the person and slowly build up to asking about mentorship.

Get started by casually asking the person to work with you on something. For example, you could go with one of the following casual requests:

- *Can I ask your advice about _____?*
- *Could I buy you a cup of coffee to discuss _____?*
- *Would you like to grab lunch on Saturday to discuss _____?*

That said, even the above questions can be too much if you're reaching out to someone who has a very limited amount of free time. Instead of asking for advice or requesting a meeting, you could ask *one simple question* to see if they respond in a positive or negative manner. From there, make a judgment call on whether a potential mentor seems willing to continue the conversation.

Another option is to closely examine the mentor's online brand. Nowadays, most experts maintain websites that link to their social media accounts, email addresses and content platforms (such as blogs, podcasts or YouTube channels). Pay close attention to these websites because they might provide an opportunity to join a potential mentor's team or become an intern in the business. Both of these options are excellent opportunities to prove yourself to a potential mentor.

#6. Grow the relationship organically.

Like every relationship, it takes time to create a solid mentorship. Keep reaching out to different experts, find ways to help them and, eventually, something will click with the right person. Keep connecting on an informal basis until you feel it's the right time to "ask" for more formal arrangement. Remember, it's a big thing to ask someone to be a mentor, so be respectful of their time and understand that not everyone will have the time (or inclination) provide this type of support.

#7. Create an informal schedule to regularly meet with your mentor.

While mentorship is less rigid than a coaching relationship, there *is* value in scheduling times to stay connected. In our busy, chaotic lives, it can be easy to go weeks without talking, so you may find scheduling meetings from time to time helpful as you establish and grow your relationship. My advice is to try to talk at least every month.

When (or where) you meet doesn't matter. You could talk over coffee or connect online for a Skype session. The important thing is to keep a consistent schedule where you regularly talk and interact with one another.

#8. Look for ways to reciprocate.

Unlike an accountabuddy, which is a reciprocal relationship, you won't be able to provide the same level of support to a mentor. It's still important to do everything you can to support this person and their work. Remember: A mentor is giving you her precious time, so you need to constantly look for ways to give back.

You should also show your appreciation by doing little things like paying for every lunch or coffee meeting, sending a gift card to the person's favorite store or restaurant, or handwriting a personalized thank-you note. Learn all you can about the person's life and look for information they will value. Giving back doesn't have to be costly, but you should do it consistently because it lets a mentor know that their time is appreciated.

Working with a mentor is a powerful form of accountability. Not only does this person *truly* understand what it takes to succeed, he or she can show you what actions you need to take on a regular basis.

Up to this point, we've talked about six types of accountability. Some might seem interesting enough to try on your own, but the challenge is knowing *where* to find people who want to achieve a similar goal. In reality, you probably don't want to approach a stranger and ask if they want to be part of a mastermind group.

Fortunately, there is a solution...

Attend conferences related to your goal.

In the next section, we talk about conferences, how they relate to accountability and the best resources for finding an event that's right for you.

Accountability Strategy #7

Attending Goal-Specific Conferences

Conferences (or live events) can become an important part of your journey toward mastering a goal. No matter what you'd like to achieve, odds are there is an event that caters to your needs.

Want to improve your gaming skills? There is the Competitive Gaming Conference in Europe. *Looking to drop your time for an important fall 10K race?* Attend one of the running summer camps offered throughout the country. Even the ultra-niche activity of basket weaving has conferences and retreats in many different states.

The benefit of attending one of these events is you'll be inspired by the people you meet and get an opportunity to improve your current set of skills. Furthermore, you can easily turn these casual interactions into lifelong friendships with people who want to form a mastermind group.

What I personally love about conferences is you tend to meet the "best of the best" of the industry. Not only do these people pay lots of money to attend the event (for the conference, flight, hotel room and food), they are also taking time from their busy schedules to meet people who share a similar goal. These are the action takers you want to meet and connect with.

For instance, I met *all* of the members of my mastermind group at a conference. We clicked during the time we spent together and later on decided to maintain what we learned by meeting on a bi-weekly basis.

While conferences are not a *direct* form of accountability, they are an important part of the process. They offer a rare opportunity to network with people who can become coaches, accountabuddies or members of a mastermind group.

All that said, conferences are not for everyone. They can be helpful if you're dedicated to achieving a goal, but they can also become a waste of time and money, so let's go over both the advantages and disadvantages of attending a live event.

Advantages:

- Great networking opportunities (if you're going to a business-related event)
- Being surrounded by like-minded people
- Building stronger connections than you can online
- Getting tips from the pros that they don't usually disclose to many people
- Easier to dedicate a few days of your time instead of meeting on a regular basis

Disadvantages:

- Can be costly because you have to pay for the event, meals, plane tickets and a hotel room
- Some events are thinly disguised "pitch fests" with low-value information and high-pressure tactics designed to talk you into buying useless products.
- Can be challenging for some people, especially introverts, to connect with others at an event where so many people are present
- You can feel rather lonely at these events if you go alone and aren't comfortable approaching people.

I feel that attending a conference can be an important part of your personal development, but it can be a waste of your time and money if you're not going with a solid game plan. In the next section, I'll go over how to maximize the value of the next conference you attend.

5 Steps to Maximize Your Next Conference

Quality is more important than quantity when attending a conference. Your goal here is twofold: First, you want to attend sessions that can help you improve your skills. Second, you want to meet people and build friendships that might turn into some form of accountability (i.e. coaching, accountabuddies or mastermind groups).

In this section, I'll go over a simple four-step plan for getting the best results from the next conference you attend.

Step #1: Identify a pool of *possible* conferences.

Getting started is really just a matter of finding an event related to a goal, buying tickets and making arrangements to travel to the event. Since we all have different goals, it would be impossible to list all the conferences you should attend. (Generally, I prefer conferences related to self-publishing and running an online business, but you probably won't be interested in them.)

Here are a few strategies for finding a conference related to your goal:

- Go to Google and type best conference [your goal] (best conference writing or best conference gaming, for example).
- Ask members of your existing network which conferences they attend or would like to attend.

- Go to your favorite virtual community and ask the same question.
- See if a local meetup group goes to a specific conference each year.
- Check out the blogs and podcasts of your favorite experts and see if they recommend a specific conference.

Create a document that includes links to conference websites, conference dates and event costs. From there, you'll get more information about each event and make a decision on the best one to attend.

Step #2: Purchase tickets to one conference.

Not every conference will specifically relate to your goal, so you should get more information about each event by looking at reviews and getting more information online.

What did people like? What did people not like? Who were the past speakers? Who is attending? How much does it cost?

Your purchasing decision will come down to many factors, but ultimately your choice should hinge on whether or not you feel the event will provide valuable information and connect you with quality people. Once you find an event that qualifies, purchase a ticket and start making travel arrangements.

Step #3: Attend important skill-specific sessions.

When you go to the event, you will be presented with a lot of material, so be sure to attend in "student mode" and take notes so you can revisit the information at a later time.

My suggestion is to download the schedule ahead of time (if possible) or grab it a day before the event starts. Examine the schedule closely, identifying the sessions you feel will be the most beneficial to you.

Honestly, these sessions will be hit or miss. I've sat through plenty of presentations that were complete wastes of my time, but there have been a few (that I initially dismissed), that turned out to be game changers for my business. So always keep an open mind and do your best to attend as many sessions as possible.

Step #4: Look for networking opportunities.

Some events will have sessions for networking or masterminding, so you can use these opportunities to connect with as many people as possible. That said, you also want to be strategic when choosing people with whom to network. Here are a few suggestions:

- **Bring business cards:** The main point of a conference is to meet new people, so you should have plenty of business cards on hand in case you want to follow up after you meet someone new (more on this later).
- **Be approachable:** Don't spend time between sessions reading or checking your mobile devices. You need to be approachable so new people are willing to talk with you.
- **Practice your elevator speech beforehand:** You should be able to introduce yourself (and your business, if you're at a business-related conference) in a few simple sentences. Practice your elevator pitch beforehand to make sure it's no more than 20 seconds long. Be sure you can deliver the speech in a straightforward manner that doesn't come across like you're trying to sell something.
- **Approach others:** Making acquaintances should be your goal at these events. I'll admit that I'm not super outgoing, but at a conference, I do make a point of approaching a few people and starting a conversation. If you are shy or introverted, it's even more important to challenge yourself to meet people, even if it makes you uncomfortable.
- **Plan meetups with online acquaintances:** If you have virtual friends, then a conference provides a great opportunity to make connections in person. You can set up an informal time to meet for a meal or drinks, or you could arrange a large meetup that includes many members of a virtual community. This is a powerful way to turn an

acquaintance into a friendship or a friendship into a weekly accountability meeting.

- **Gain visibility:** It is easy to get lost in the crowd at an event. To *really* get the most out of an event, you could offer to be a presenter, facilitator or volunteer. Asking smart questions is a great way to gain visibility. Doing so creates additional training opportunities and makes people want to learn more about you. Some of the best training comes from the questions asked by event participants, so don't be afraid to speak up.
- **Choose the right sessions:** Not only do you want to hear information that interests you, but you want to meet attendees who are interested in similar information.
- **Don't drink excessively:** Having a beer or two at dinner is perfectly fine, but avoid getting hammered and making a fool of yourself with people you've just met.

You don't necessarily have to do everything on this list, but try to be as proactive as possible to make connections with the other people at the conference.

Step #5: Follow up with every person.

It is essential that you follow up with the people you meet within a week of the conference. You could email them, connect on social media or even give them a call. *How* you connect is irrelevant. What's important is you actually do it.

A great strategy for reconnecting with new acquaintances is to use the business cards people give you at each event. When you receive one, step aside after the conversation ends and take a few notes about the person on the back. Include any personal information or ideas for connecting with that person.

If a new contact has a wife named Mary and two kids, write a note that says, "I hope Mary and the kids are doing well." This personalized touch is a great way to deepen a relationship.

This isn't a Machiavellian strategy. You're simply contacting someone you liked meeting and would like to talk to in the future.

Okay, those are the seven ways you can add accountability to your life. To recap, you can get feedback and gain motivation to work on a goal by:

1) Using a mobile app.
2) Joining a virtual community.
3) Working with an accountabuddy.
4) Forming a mastermind group.
5) Working with a coach.
6) Meeting with a mentor.
7) Attending goal-specific conferences.

As you can see, there are several forms of accountability. You could do anything from updating a mobile app on a daily basis all the way to working with a coach to help you master a goal. Each option presents an opportunity to make a powerful change in your life—but they're not "one-size-fits-all" solutions. That's why you need to understand *where* you are in life, *what* type of help you need, *how* to get started and what to do *when* things don't go according to plan. And that's what we'll cover in the final section of this book.

PART IV

CONCLUSION

How to Add Accountability to Your Goals

Throughout this book, we've covered a number of strategies for adding accountability on your path to achieving a goal. We all have different things we want to achieve. This means if a strategy works for others, it might not be beneficial for you. That's why you need an action plan that fits your busy schedule and helps you identify which strategy will work best for you.

In this section, we take everything you've learned and turn it into a six-step process that helps you be accountable on a daily basis.

Step #1: Evaluate your needs.

Depending on the goal, your level of experience will be different from others'. You might need a *little* help in one area and a *lot* of help in another. As such, each major goal you have will require its own type of accountability.

For instance, I have many goals related to my online business, where I'm required to constantly learn and implement new strategies. As such, I meet with both an accountabuddy and a mastermind group because these weekly conversations keep my head in the game and reinforce the idea that I should always continue to grow.

On the other hand, I have a lower accountability threshold for exercising and writing. I don't need a lot of motivation to stick to these habits. Really, my only form of accountability is to use Coach.me to track these activities on a daily basis.

You can use accountability in a variety of ways. Unfortunately, this means it's tempting to try to do everything all at once.

My suggestion is to identify the goal that requires the most assistance and work on that first. This goal should relate directly to a habit you can do on a daily basis. If all you need is a little reinforcement, then a virtual community or mobile app will probably do the trick. However, if you feel the goal requires a major improvement to a specific skill, then you should consider hiring a coach.

Step #2: Take an honest look at your schedule.

In addition to evaluating your needs, it's equally important to be honest about your schedule. If you're already pressed for time and never have a spare moment, then it's unlikely you can commit to a regular meeting.

What you could do *instead* is exchange updates with an accountabuddy via emails or text messages.

Be honest about your time. Nobody can do it all. It's better to recognize ahead of time that your time is rather limited than to start a regular meeting and then quit after a few weeks.

Step #3: Focus on one habit at a time.

In the book *Willpower* by Roy F. Baumeister and John Tierney, the authors talked about a concept known as "ego depletion," which is "a person's diminished capacity to regulate their thoughts, feelings, and actions."

The basic premise is that willpower is like a muscle that weakens as it's used throughout the day. We don't have a limitless supply of willpower; once we've used up our supply for the day, it's gone. At that point, it becomes very hard to exercise discipline.

Ego depletion impacts our ability to form new habits because our supply of willpower is spread out among all areas of our lives.

Because of this, it's important to work on only one habit at a time. That way, your store of willpower can be channeled into completing that one habit, increasing the odds of success.

The point of mentioning ego depletion here is to help you understand that you won't successfully add accountability to your week if you're also trying to add dozens of other habits. (This is the reason why most people fail with their New Year's resolutions.) Instead of trying to do it all, you should *pick one accountability habit* and completely focus on it.

Is it a weekly mastermind meeting? Will you track a set of daily habits with Coach.me? Are you contacting a few people every day in order to land a mentor?

Identify your habit now and structure your day around doing it on a continuous basis. Whether it is stepping out to get a coach or committing to post on your virtual community once a day, decide what this one activity will be to get you started.

Step #4: Make a commitment for 30 days.

Some people say it takes 21 days to build a habit, while others claim it takes up to 66 days. The truth is, the length of time really varies from person to person and habit to habit. You'll find that some habits are easy to build, while others require more effort. My advice is to commit to a single habit for the next 30 days (or a month, to keep it simple). During this time, your entire life should be structured around the completion of this one action, regardless of what life throws your way.

Step #5: Take baby steps as you build up the accountability habit.

Really, the only way to make a habit stick is to turn it into an automatic behavior. You can do this by taking baby steps and creating a low level of commitment. The idea here is to create a commitment so small that it's impossible to fail (a micro-commitment). It's more important to stay consistent and not miss a day than it is to hit a specific milestone. When you have a low level of commitment, you'll find it easier to get started.

Let's say you want to build accountability through a virtual community. These are some of the steps you'd have to take to reach your goal:

- Pick a social media site and log in to the site every day.
- Search the site for groups related to your goal and add the top candidates to a "short list."
- Go through your short list and pick one group to join and participate in.
- Join the group, read the rules and check out previous threads to better understand the members.
- Create a five-minute daily habit of checking into this group and reading new posts.
- Look for valuable information from outside sources and use it to spark conversation.

It's not hard to turn accountability into a daily action plan—even if you have a limited amount of time. Simply think of the end goal and reverse engineer all the steps necessary to get you there. Then create a step-by-step plan you can work on in small chunks.

Step #6: Make an if-then plan for possible obstacles.

Every goal *will* have obstacles—especially when you're building a habit that relies on other people (like you would with accountability). The trick is to identify any potential challenges ahead of time and make a plan for how you'll handle them.

My suggestion is to think of a series of "if-then statements" that identify potential challenges and the actions you will take to overcome them.

Here are some examples of if-then statements you could use to overcome your obstacles:

"If I miss more than one mastermind meeting a month, then I will evaluate my schedule and make sure it's at a time that I can always make."

"If I frequently fall short of my accountability statement goals, then I will evaluate what I promise to do each week and create more realistic goals."

"If someone frequently misses meetings or does not participate fully in mastermind meetings, then I will speak to them privately or search for a replacement member."

"If a member of my mastermind group consistently doesn't reach his goals, then I will be honest in my feedback and give advice he can immediately implement."

One of my favorite quotes is, *"The only certainty is that nothing is certain."*

You should constantly think of how a goal can be derailed and come up with a possible solution in case these challenges come to fruition. Only then will you truly be in a position to expect the unexpected.

And since we're on the subject of challenges, it's important to have an action plan for those times when you fail or you're almost about to give up. In the next (and final) section, I'll go over a few a simple plans for maintaining consistency with this strategy.

What to Do When Accountability Fails

In a perfect world, when you add accountability to your goals, you get *exactly* what you need, when you need it. You grow leaps and bounds in your personal development, meet your important goals and build life-long relationships with like-minded, awesome people.

Unfortunately, we don't live in a perfect world.

Instead, there will be many obstacles that *might* prevent you from consistently being accountable in your life.

That's when the excuses often come in:

"I joined a mastermind group, but nobody made the time to show up."

"My accountabuddy turned out to be a jerk, so I'm just going to work on my goals on my own!"

"I don't have time for dealing with other people's issues in an accountability group; I just need to worry about myself."

"My coach doesn't understand my business. He often has me work on tasks that aren't directly related to my goals."

Here's the thing... accountability isn't a magic wand.

It's flawed, like everything else in life.

You *should* expect to encounter challenges, failures and frustrations. Perhaps they will make you want to give up or use self-justification to talk yourself out of continuing with this strategy.

Self-justification is when you start to make excuses for your actions. Specifically, you look for *reasons why* accountability won't work for you. The excuses may seem valid, but in reality, they're poison to the goals you've created for yourself.

Ideally, when you start making self-justification statements, it's the job of your mastermind group, accountabuddy, coach or mentor to call you out on these negative thoughts. That said, I think it's more important to remember the first lesson from this book—take 100 percent responsibility for your life.

Being 100 percent responsible means you ignore self-justification statements and avoid making excuses about it being someone else's fault that you're not achieving a specific goal.

My advice is to carefully examine any accountability-specific problem and look for a possible solution.

Here are a few examples:

Problem: "I didn't know *how* to do a specific goal for this week, so I never got around to doing it."

Solution: It's important to remember that an accountability goal should be actionable. If you don't know how to do something, then craft a statement like "This week, I will spend 10 hours researching possible strategies to achieve this goal."

Problem: "I worked really hard this week, and I was productive with other projects, but I didn't achieve my accountability statements for the week."

Solution: It may be that your accountability statement is too ambitious. Such a projection should push you, but it needs to be doable within the allotted time. When creating an accountability statement, always consider any personal obligations, appointments, possible emergencies and work-related activities such as meetings or email overload. It's okay to miss an occasional goal, but if it has become a pattern, then you need to rethink what you're agreeing to do on a weekly basis.

Problem: "In the three weeks since my last mastermind group meeting, I forgot about the accountability statement and didn't remember to do it."

Solution: Accountability should be tied directly to a short-term goal, but it will be hard to work on it if you're not meeting with others on a regular basis. My advice is to meet *at least* bi-weekly with your mastermind group or accountabuddy. That way, your short-term objectives will always be on your mind and you'll be focused enough to remember to work on them.

Problem: "The week started well, but then there was the playoff game, *Daredevil* on Netflix and I just had to wash my cat..."

Solution: At the risk of sounding harsh, achieving major goals requires discipline. Sure, you might miss a fun activity from time to time, but you should also look at the bigger picture and think of what it would be like to complete an important life goal. Odds are, the activity you sacrificed will pale in comparison to what you truly want to achieve.

Problem: "I'm not getting results from my mastermind group because one member keeps interrupting the discussion and rarely adds value."

Solution: Meet with the other members and be candid about this person. If they agree that this person is a disruptive force, then either talk to the person and give him one last chance *or* make the difficult decision to replace him with someone who does add value.

Problem: "I learn a lot from my mastermind meeting, but I am uncomfortable with the 'hot seat' format."

Solution: Usually, with time, the fear of the "hot seat" will diminish. This usually happens once you've grown comfortable with the members of your group. Furthermore, the hot seat provides an opportunity you shouldn't pass up. While there is a lot to learn by sharing ideas with other members, you can gain a lot of value by being brave enough to open yourself to honest and direct feedback. Sure, some comments will sting, but remember that the people giving feedback are doing it to help you grow as a person.

Problem: "My time to talk is limited, and I rarely get a chance to talk about my specific solutions."

Solution: This often happens when there is a lack of authority from the group facilitator. This person needs to be tough with other members and make sure that everyone stays on topic and keeps comments brief and to the point.

Also, the group might be too large. One solution is to poll all the members, find out who is truly committed to the process and then encourage anyone who seems uncertain to either make a firm commitment or leave the group. In my opinion, sometimes you need to a little bit of culling in order to transform a lackluster gathering of people into a results-driven mastermind group.

Problem: "My coach rarely provides feedback or information I can use to improve my goals."

Solution: This one is simple. If you're not getting results from a coach (as long as you're taking action on their advice), then you should immediately fire this person and look for someone who can help you.

Accountability can become a powerful mechanism for achieving major goals, but it also comes with its own unique set of challenges. That said, if you're willing to take the time to think of solutions to these obstacles, you'll find it's not that hard to overcome anything that crosses your path.

Well, that's almost it for *Crowdsource Your Success*.

But, before you go, allow to me to end with a few parting words...

Final Thoughts

Throughout this book, we have talked about the many aspects of accountability—what is required, how to get it and what to do with it. There are many different ways to take action on this strategy, but what you do really depends on *your individual needs*. You must take a hard look at your goals and determine the best way to reach them.

The main premise of this book is to teach you the importance of taking personal responsibility for your goals *and* surrounding yourself with people who can lend assistance during this unique journey.

Remember these important benefits of accountability:

- If your motivation is lacking, there are people who can encourage and inspire you.
- If an obstacle pops up unexpectedly, there are people who can provide possible solutions.
- If don't know how to do something, there are people who can either teach it to you or recommend a resource for getting started.

When you have a powerful network at your disposal, you'll find that it's not hard to find *someone* who has the ability to help you get through any situation.

Now it's time for you to take the reins and use accountability to reach your goals.

Just remember one thing...

To achieve a goal, not only do you need to take 100% responsibility for your results, you also need constant feedback from others to help you along the way.

For some people, using a mobile app is all it takes to stay accountable. Other people need ongoing guidance and support from coaches or mentors. There's no right or wrong way to implement this strategy. The most important thing is to use *some* form of accountability to improve your life.

I wish you the best of luck!

Steve "S.J." Scott

www.DevelopGoodHabits.com

Would You Like to Know More?

You can learn a lot more about habit development in my other Kindle books. The best part? I frequently run special promotions where I offer free or discounted books (usually $0.99) on Amazon.

One way to get <u>instant notifications</u> for these deals is to subscribe to my email list. By joining not only will you receive updates on the latest offer, you'll also get a free copy of the "Bad Habits No More" audio package. Check out the below link to learn more.

Go Here to Get Updates on Free and $0.99 Kindle Books:

<u>www.developgoodhabits.com/free-70hh</u>

More Books by S.J. Scott

- *10-Minute Declutter: The Stress-Free Habit for Simplifying Your Home*

- *Exercise Enough: 32 Tactics for Building the Exercise Habit (Even If You Hate Working Out)*

- *Confident You: An Introvert's Guide to Success in Life and Business*

- *The Daily Entrepreneur: 33 Success Habits for Small Business Owners, Freelancers and Aspiring 9-to-5 Escape Artists*

- *Level Up Your Day: How to Maximize the 6 Essential Areas of Your Daily Routine*

- *Master Evernote: The Unofficial Guide to Organizing Your Life with Evernote (Plus 75 Ideas for Getting Started)*

- *Bad Habits No More: 25 Steps to Break ANY Bad Habit*

- *Habit Stacking: 97 Small Life Changes That Take Five Minutes or Less*

- *To-Do List Makeover: A Simple Guide to Getting the Important Things Done*

- *23 Anti-Procrastination Habits: How to Stop Being Lazy and Get Results in Your Life*

- *S.M.A.R.T. Goals Made Simple: 10 Steps to Master Your Personal and Career Goals*

- *115 Productivity Apps to Maximize Your Time: Apps for iPhone, iPad, Android, Kindle Fire and PC/iOS Desktop Computers*

- *Writing Habit Mastery: How to Write 2,000 Words a Day and Forever Cure Writer's Block*

- *Declutter Your Inbox: 9 Proven Steps to Eliminate Email Overload*

- *Wake Up Successful: How to Increase Your Energy and Achieve Any Goal with a Morning Routine*

- *10,000 Steps Blueprint: The Daily Walking Habit for Healthy Weight Loss and Lifelong Fitness*

- *70 Healthy Habits: How to Eat Better, Feel Great, Get More Energy and Live a Healthy Lifestyle*

- *Resolutions That Stick! How 12 Habits Can Transform Your New Year*

All books can be found at: <u>www.DevelopGoodHabits.com</u>

About the Author

In his books, S.J. Scott provides daily action plans for every area of your life: health, fitness, work and personal relationships. Unlike other personal development guides, his content focuses on taking action. So instead of reading over-hyped strategies that rarely work in the real-world, you'll get information that can be immediately implemented.

51308651R00083

Made in the USA
Middletown, DE
01 July 2019

5 Real-World Examples of Accountability

When people hear terms like "coaching," "mentoring" and "masterminds," they often think about these concepts in relation to the business world, but this kind of support can also have a positive impact on personal growth. The goal of this section is to show you how accountability can improve *any* area of your life. More specifically, I'll go over five types of groups that provide a high level of accountability.

Some of these examples might be familiar, but there will be some that you may not have considered. To start, I would like to talk briefly about one of the best tools for finding like-minded people in your area.

How to Use Meetup.com

There are *many* types of accountability groups. The trick is to find ones in your area, which is why I recommend Meetup.com.

Meetup.com is used by people all over the world to find local groups based on a specific interest. Simply enter your town, ZIP code, state or country, and you'll get a complete list of the "meetups" in your area.

Meetups are great because they are local and target people with specific goals or common interests. More often than not, the people you meet will become close friends. Joining a Meetup.com group gives you the opportunity to work on your goals while having fun at the same time.

The biggest drawback of using Meetup.com is that you might have difficulty finding a local group that matches your interests. If you live in a city and you're interested in left-handed basket weaving, you can probably find a group of left-handed basket weavers, but you might be out of luck if you live in a rural area.

If you *can't* find a specific group, then it's easy to start your own meetup. You'd be surprised at how many people wait for someone else to take action. If you form your own group, odds are there will be people who want to join.

For instance, my friend Kristen wanted to be part of a low-key running group in her area, but couldn't find one she liked. So she created her own, which she calls the <u>Calf Burn Addiction Society</u>. This informal group has turned into a powerful example of accountability where members meet for runs, volunteer at races and do other fun activities together.

Whether you join an existing Meetup group or start your own, Meetup.com is the first place to look if you want to join a group full of people who share a similar goal. With that in mind, let's go over the five examples of how accountability can help with your personal development.

Example#1: Skill Improvement

Just about any goal you can think of has a group, either locally or nationally, you can use to get feedback, improve your skills and learn about valuable resources.

Let's go over a few examples:

Toastmasters International: This nonprofit educational organization operates clubs worldwide for the purpose of helping members improve their communication, public speaking and leadership skills.

If you have a goal to improve your public speaking skills, Toastmasters provides a supportive, learn-by-doing environment that can help you improve the way you communicate. Not only do you get instant feedback on your speeches, each local club has a treasure trove of resources designed to improve your weakest areas.